KEY CONCEPTS IN CONTEMPORARY POPULAR FICTION

Key Concepts in Literature

Published titles
Key Concepts in Literary Theory, 3rd edition
Julian Wolfreys et al.

Key Concepts in Contemporary Popular Fiction
Bernice M. Murphy

Forthcoming titles
Key Concepts in the Gothic
William Hughes

Key Concepts in Contemporary Popular Fiction

Bernice M. Murphy

EDINBURGH
University Press

Edinburgh University Press is one of the leading university presses in the UK. We publish academic books and journals in our selected subject areas across the humanities and social sciences, combining cutting-edge scholarship with high editorial and production values to produce academic works of lasting importance. For more information visit our website: edinburghuniversitypress.com

Edinburgh University Press Ltd
The Tun – Holyrood Road
12(2f) Jackson's Entry
Edinburgh EH8 8PJ

Typeset in Sabon by
Servis Filmsetting Ltd, Stockport, Cheshire
and printed and bound in Great Britain by
CPI Group (UK) Ltd, Croydon CR0 4YY

A CIP record for this book is available from the British Library

ISBN 978 1 4744 1103 5 (hardback)
ISBN 978 1 4744 1104 2 (webready PDF)
ISBN 978 1 4744 1105 9 (paperback)
ISBN 978 1 4744 1106 6 (epub)

Contents

Acknowledgements

I would like to begin by thanking Jackie Jones at EUP for asking me to write this volume in the first place: it's been a fantastic opportunity. The continued support and encouragement of my colleagues in the TCD School of English, and in particular, Stephen Matterson, Darryl Jones, Helen Conrad O'Briain and Diane Sadler, is also very much appreciated. I was able to write much of this book during a period of study leave granted by the college in 2015, for which I am very grateful. The students from the MPhil in Popular Literature and my 'Contemporary Popular Literature' class frequently served as test subjects for some of the material published here: their good-natured enthusiasm was always heartening and illuminating. As ever, my family and friends were patient and supportive, even when pushed to the limits of sanity by my constant mutterings about zombies, mass culture and Amazon. com. This book is dedicated to my fellow 'Pop Lit' lecturers Clare Clarke, Jarlath Killeen and Elizabeth McCarthy. They are excellent academics, even better colleagues and valued friends.

Bernice M. Murphy, Trinity College Dublin

Introduction

Key Concepts in Contemporary Popular Fiction is intended to serve as an accessible starting point for students, scholars and general readers looking for an authoritative and concise introduction to this increasingly significant field of literary study. It provides a succinct overview of the most significant critical terms and theoretical approaches used within popular fiction studies at the present time. Because the focus here is also on the contemporary, particular effort has been made to provide an insight into trends and terms related to twenty-first-century popular fiction. However, one cannot understand the current state of popular fiction without also engaging with the prior historical, cultural, commercial and academic contexts of the subject area, and so these elements have also been taken into consideration.

Before outlining the structure of this volume in more detail, it is important briefly to outline just what we mean by the term 'popular fiction' in the first place. This is actually a slightly trickier task that you might initially think. As David Glover and Scott McCracken put it:

> 'Popular fiction' is a deceptively simple phrase, at once indispensable and commonplace, yet often left unsettlingly vague. One of the problems with finding a clear definition of popular fiction is that the subject of study is not always clear. The cultural formation designated by 'popular fiction' has changed over time and varies according to its cultural and geographical situation. (2012: 1)

The most straightforward understanding of the term, as has often rightly been pointed out, is to take it as meaning 'fiction that is popular' – as opposed to works of fiction that remain unread by the vast majority of the reading public (see, for instance, Ashley 1997: 2; Berberich 2015: 2; Glover and McCracken 2012: 1; Gelder 2004: 20; and McCracken 1998: 1).

However, there are problems with this definition. As Ken Gelder puts it, 'Authors of literary fiction can have bestsellers, too, and conversely, not every work of popular fiction sells successfully' (2004: 3). Indeed, some novels categorised as 'literary' rather than 'popular' fiction do achieve a wide readership and considerable commercial success (and here, works by authors such as Hilary Mantel, Ian McEwan, Donna Tartt and Jonathan Franzen come to mind). Then there is the fact that as the melancholy remainders section of any major bookshop, or the lowest ranks of the Amazon.com sales ranking system will attest, there are many works of popular fiction that don't find many readers or sell many copies. So this is why thinking of 'popularity' primarily in terms of sales, or commercial visibility, is a mistake, even if consideration of these factors is still an important facet of the study of popular fiction.

Another way critics and academics have discussed the meaning of the term 'popular fiction' is to relate it to the assumed audience these kinds of texts attract. For instance, Christina Berberich, echoing Glover and McCracken, rightly notes that 'the term "popular" contains a variety of different, and potentially contradictory, meanings, and is one weighed down with ideological meaning' (2015: 3). She then cites pioneering cultural studies critic Raymond Williams, who in his 1976 book *Keywords: A Vocabulary of Culture and Society*, 'defines "popular" as, historically, "belonging to the people," "widely favoured" or "well liked" but points out that it has always held the connotation of being "low" or "base" [. . .]' (2015: 3). Williams himself continues:

> Popular was being seen from the point of view of the people rather than from those seeking favour or power over them. Yet the earlier sense has not died. **Popular culture** was not identified *by the people* but by others, and it still carries two older senses: inferior kinds of work (c.f. **popular literature, popular press** as distinguished from *quality press*); and work deliberately setting out to win favour (**popular journalism** as distinguished from *democratic journalism*, or **popular entertainment**): as well as the more modern sense of being liked by many people, with which, of course, in many cases, the earlier senses overlap. (1983: 237, emphasis in original)

This definition is important for us here not only because it refers to the long-standing association between the 'popular' and cultural products which are of poor quality, and pander to the lowest common denominator, it also emphasises the link between the 'popular' and the widest possible audience. Popular fiction has often been associated with the 'common people', and hence with the 'lower' or 'working' classes, as well as the ever-widening ranks of the middle classes, in large part because of the real-life historical development of this form of literature. As Clive Bloom has observed, the development of genre fiction in the UK is inherently linked to the advent of mass literacy in the late nineteenth century. 'The market amongst lower-middle class and working-class readers was effectively created when rising incomes, increasing leisure, and greater national cohesion aligned with reasonable levels of reading ability' (2008: 45). An earlier critic of popular fiction, Victor Neuburg, also noted that the 'progressive growth of the reading public' had begun by the end of the eighteenth century, and that the age of 'mass-produced literature' had begun by end of the nineteenth (1977: 15). Back in 1957, Margaret Dalziel began her study of mid-Victorian popular fiction by arguing that the increasing literacy during this period had created an avid audience of 'lower class people', many of whom 'lived lives of unspeakable degradation'. She continued, 'What they wanted was not cheap knowledge but cheap amusement, not information but fiction', thereby suggesting that this kind of fiction was primarily a kind of tawdry distraction for those occupying the lowest rungs of Victorian society (12).

However, as the Key Critical and Theoretical Approaches section of this volume will demonstrate, it is not only the working-class relationship with popular fiction that has attracted scholarly interest (and, frequently, concern and even outright disapproval): the likes of Matthew Arnold, Q. D. Leavis, F. R. Leavis, Dwight Macdonald, Pierre Bourdieu and, more recently, cultural critics such as Curtis White and Chris Hedges, have also discussed the impact that they see popular reading material and 'mass culture' having upon the middle-class audience as well.

In the late-twentieth and twenty-first centuries, however, it becomes clear that despite this longstanding historical association with the working class in particular, readers of popular fiction can and do belong to every social class, income and education level, although the question of who, exactly, constitutes the main readership of *particular* genres does significantly vary depending on what genre one is referring to. Furthermore, as the emergence of self-publishing and digital distribution platforms contributes to an ever more expansive marketplace in which the idea of specific narratives calibrated to the reading preferences and prejudices of the individual reader becomes increasingly achievable, the question of *who* reads *what* kind of genre fiction (and for what reasons) becomes all the complex. It is more helpful then for the critic of contemporary popular fiction, as Scott McCracken presciently suggested back in 1998, to look instead 'at the relationship between a particular audience (or coalition of reader groups) and a particular text or genre' (5) rather than try to make overly broad conclusions about the readership of popular fiction in general.

This is all very well, but it still leaves the question of 'What is popular fiction?' hanging. Thankfully, the critical consensus of the last couple of decades has arrived at some broad points of general agreement, which I have summarised below in eight key points.

1. Works of Popular Fiction are Aimed at a General Audience

It can be taken as a given that a work of popular fiction has been expressly written for a general rather than an elite audience (in contrast with literary fiction, which, as we shall see in the Key Critical and Theoretical Approaches section, has often been associated with an 'elite' and 'cultivated' minority). 'A writer produces popular fiction because he or she intends (or would prefer) to reach a large number of readers,' Gelder argues (2004: 22). Accessibility, affordability and commercial availability are also considered to be important associated aspects of the 'popular' text: it stands to reason that in order to reach a general audience, a text should have a high degree of that hard-to-define but important quality known as 'readability', and that it should not be prohibitively priced or impossible to find.

2. Popular Fiction is Entertaining and Escapist

It has often been asserted that popular fiction's primary purpose is to *entertain*. Literary fiction has many times been described as 'serious' fiction, a description that often brings with it the unspoken assumption that popular fiction is essentially 'unserious', i.e. frivolous, light-weight and intellectually unfulfilling – the literary equivalent of high-calorie, low-quality fast food. It has also long been common to refer to popular fiction's appeal in terms that emphasise its explicitly escapist, supposedly 'drug-like' qualities. When readers and critics refer to a work of fiction as a 'compulsive read', or a 'page turner', or describe themselves as 'devouring' a new novel, or 'losing themselves' in a story, they are highlighting the connection between engaging with a popular text and the desire to temporarily escape from the 'real' world. One of the attractions of digital publishing is that it facilitates instant access to an author's back catalogue, a technological innovation which not only privileges the 'impulse' buy, but which also enables the kind of 'binge' more commonly associated with the online streaming of TV shows. It is precisely this kind of immersive and diverting quality that represents one of popular fiction's most engaging and remarked upon characteristics.

3. Popular Fiction is Easy to Identify

Works of popular fiction can almost always be quickly assigned to a particular generic category, or categories. Indeed, 'popular fiction' and 'genre fiction' are now often said to be essentially the same thing, even though the commercial classification of popular fiction into a specific 'genre system' (as we would recognise it today) didn't really get under way until the late nineteenth century (Glover and McCracken 2012: 28; Pittard 2015: 12). What this means is when a reader picks up a work of popular fiction, be it a crime novel, a mystery or a romance, they have certain pre-existing expectations about the basic character types and plot elements that it will contain. As Gelder puts it, 'with popular fiction, generic identities are always visible' (2004: 42). This generic visibility even extends to the presentation of the novel in question itself: when it comes to popular fiction, you really can usually judge a book by its cover.

As well as having cover art that tends to encourage certain generic expectations (for instance, it has often been noted that Chick-Lit covers often have 'frothy' covers which emphasise accessories such as shoes and handbags), novels categorised as 'genre fiction' tend to be displayed alongside volumes belonging to the same genre or sub-genre in book stores (be they online or physical), often have the name of the genre itself written on the spine or on the cover, and frequently have their generic identity clearly identified in the blurb and other marketing materials (e.g. 'A heart-stopping thriller in the tradition of *The Silence of the Lambs*'). Interestingly, our expectations and prior familiarity with plot elements, themes or tropes do not interfere with our enjoyment of the text (unless it fails to engage or satisfy us for some reason). Popular fiction therefore gratifies in part because it provides us with what we want, or, as some critics would argue, with what we have been conditioned to *think* we want.

4. Popular Fiction Doesn't Have to be Particularly Original

The moment that a genre novel achieves a certain level of critical and commercial success, it will almost certainly inspire a host of imitators. This was the case even in the early days: in 1764, Horace Walpole's *The Castle of Otranto* created the blueprint for the gothic genre. Within a matter of months, a rash of texts 'inspired' by *Otranto* had begun to appear (Jane Austen even mocks some of them in her satirical 1817 novel *Northanger Abbey*). Publishers and authors have therefore always reasonably assumed that if the readers have lapped up one kind of novel, they will probably be interested in three more just like it. For instance, the success of Gillian Flynn's 2012 bestseller *Gone Girl* on both sides of the Atlantic meant that within a year or so, domestic thrillers about unreliable women trapped in unfulfilling or dangerous relationships had become a staple of the bestseller lists. Many of them also had the word 'girl' in the title, despite the fact that almost all of these books revolve around the domestic travails of grown women (for this trend, we can also thank Stieg Larsson). Even though many of these novels were no doubt written (or at least planned) before Flynn's book achieved cultural ubiquity, publishers were happy to make sure that they were marketed and packaged in such a way as to springboard off her success, sometimes spectacularly so: in 2015 Paula Hawkins's *The Girl on the Train* actually beat *Gone Girl*'s sales in both the US and UK. Similarly, huge sales for *Fifty Shades of Grey* in 2011 and 2012 resulted in the release of a flood of erotic novels with similarly monochrome covers. Compounding the feedback loop of pop fiction influence was the fact that E. L. James's series had itself had started life as *Twilight* fanfiction. One hit will always inspire another.

5. Popular Fiction is Plot Driven

One of the characteristics often said to distinguish popular fiction from literary fiction is the fact that plot is always more important than language, style or tone. It is not uncommon for a work of literary fiction to feature a plot in which, on the surface, not all that much happens. However, a work of popular fiction in which plot is entirely secondary to stylistic concerns would, however, likely be considered a disappointment by most readers. Popular novels are frequently crammed with incident, and often have complicated, intricate plots (this particularly is the case with certain genres in particular, such as the thriller, which thrives on narrative reversals and twists). This is certainly *not* to say, however, that a work of popular fiction cannot have distinctive language or tonal and stylistic characteristics (as the often parodied – because they are so recognisable – examples of authors such as Raymond Chandler, H. P. Lovecraft and Dan Brown amply demonstrate).

6. Popular Fiction is Shaped by Commercial and Technological Considerations

Commercial, industrial and technological factors are always key components in the creation, distribution, reception and analysis of popular fiction (to characterise literary fiction as being entirely unaffected by these factors would be inaccurate, but they are generally understood to be less significant). Popular fiction as we understand it today would not exist had it not been for the introduction in the eighteenth and nineteenth centuries of cheaper and more efficient publication technologies which facilitated the production and distribution of affordable reading materials targeted at the widest audience possible. Similarly, the post-1930s 'paperback revolution' also owed much to advances in printing technology, wider distribution channels and reductions in the price of paper.

The last decade has seen another revolution in popular fiction brought about by the advent of digital publishing and the rapid proliferation of online publication and distribution venues, as well as the arrival of more affordable and efficient e-reading devices. However, in yet another sign of the fast-moving nature of the industry, these have already been displaced, with current industry trends showing that younger readers prefer to read their e-books on apps downloaded to multi-purpose devices such as tablets and smart phones. The writing, marketing, selling and distribution of popular fiction in both hard copy and electronic format has also been profoundly affected by the commercial dominance of one company in particular, Amazon.com. To fully engage with the subject area, one must therefore be aware of these historical, industrial and commercial trends.

7. Popular Fiction is Ephemeral

Shaped as it is by the ever-shifting tides of popular taste, the landscape of popular fiction is a constantly evolving one. Although the general outlines of most of today's major genres were by and large established before the end of the Victorian era (although they would all undergo significant reconfigurations in the twentieth century), specific fads and fashions will always arise in response to particular historical and cultural moments. Just as established genres and sub-genres can fall out of fashion – the Western is often cited as the most notable example – so too can new ones emerge (although they are almost always recognisably derived from existing genres). Two of the most notable recent examples include 'Cli-Fi', or 'Climate Change Fiction', a science fiction sub-genre focusing on the causes, effects and consequences of environmental catastrophe, and the post-2000 rise to commercial prominence of Urban Fantasy, which combines elements of fantasy, horror, noir and adventure. As the emergence of 'Cli-Fi' in particular suggests, popular fiction can and does evolve in response to pressing contemporary anxieties and real-world events. Furthermore, whilst publishing trends and reader preferences may wax and wane over the decades, as Gary Hoppenstand argues, the transitory qualities of these kinds of fictions are also significantly 'mitigated by a number of powerful narrative storylines that have survived the historical eras of their invention to become part of the larger collective social consciousness, not only reflecting our attitudes and beliefs (about such concepts as love, heroism and death), but influencing them as well' (2016: 119).

8. Popular Fiction is Part of the Wider Landscape of Popular Culture

Popular fiction has always had a symbiotic relationship with other forms of popular culture, and no study of popular fiction can – or should – entirely divorce itself from these contexts. Indeed, many of the most significant post-1960s discussions of popular fiction were conducted by academics who were operating from within a cultural studies or communication studies perspective rather than as literary scholars (although this has changed in recent years). In addition, as Scott McCracken has noted, 'Contemporary popular fiction is the product of a huge entertainment industry. Written fiction is only part of that industry, which markets and sells popular narratives for film, radio, television and periodicals as well as in book form. To study popular fiction is to study only a small part of popular culture' (1998: 1). There has always been considerable cross-fertilisation between popular fiction and other forms of popular culture. Best-selling popular novels were frequently (and not always with the author's permission) adapted for the stage in the eighteenth and nineteenth centuries: film adaptations of popular novels have been a staple of the cinema since the very beginnings of the medium, and radio plays, television shows and pop songs have all influenced (or been influenced by) popular fiction.

To cite one recent example of this kind of movement between mediums: the past decade has seen the emergence of the superhero narrative as one of the most ubiquitous trends in contemporary popular culture. The international box-office has been dominated by Marvel properties since *Iron Man* was released in 2008, and now there are a whole raft of superhero TV films and shows based on both Marvel and DC characters, some aimed at the more 'family friendly' section of the audience, some carefully calibrated for a more self-consciously 'mature' demographic.

There has also been a significant but, to date, rather overlooked popular fiction component to this trend: dozens of novels based on both existing and original characters have been published in the past decade. In short, a variety of pop culture narrative previously most commonly associated with the comic book/graphic novel only (albeit incorrectly, as there had been superhero radio shows, serials and cartoons since the 1940s) has made the transition to mainstream pop-culture ubiquity on the big screen, the small screen and the bookshelves, and the relationship between these properties remains a deeply symbiotic one, even when the novels concerned involve entirely original characters and scenarios (as many of them do).

The Internet age has also brought with it a whole new adjunct to the entertainment industry. Blogs, Twitter feeds, Facebook pages and online review sites such as Goodreads and Amazon customer reviews facilitate rapid access to a broad spectrum of reader and critical reactions to a particular work. The emergence of a multitude of social media and blogging platforms has also assisted the dissemination of feminist, LGBTQ and racially conscious critiques of popular fiction that can now reach a much wider (and more receptive) audience than would have been the case in the past. Readers and authors whose own racial, national and gender identities may not previously have been reflected in 'mainstream' popular fiction also now have the potential ability to reach a much wider audience, although the publishing industry as a whole remains quite conservative.

In recent years, podcasting has also become an increasingly important medium for pop fiction storytelling, with the likes of the surreal serial *Welcome to Night Vale* (2012–) spawning both a novel and a live stage show, as well as helping to create an audience for a host of other genre podcasts in 2015 and 2016. In another sign that popular fiction (like writing in general) continues to evolve beyond the boundaries of the traditional, hard-copy book format, it was reported in 2016 that audio books represent one of the major future growth areas for the publishing industry. Video games have become an ever more significant and sophisticated storytelling medium, and many gamers now argue, with considerable justification, that titles such as *Bioshock* (2007), *The Last of Us* (2013) and *Fallout 4* (2015) are just as immersive and imaginative as any novel or film. The pending arrival of a new generation of virtual reality headsets (such as the Oculus Rift) will no doubt once again radically reconfigure our ideas of what popular narrative can and should achieve, and encourage further consideration of the relationship between the world of print (which now of course encompasses both traditional hardcopy and e-book format) and other forms of entertainment.

Before briefly discussing the structure and remit of this volume, it is important to emphasise the reasons why the academic study of popular fiction is a worthwhile endeavour. Whilst it will come as no surprise to find a robust defence of the subject area in a book devoted to the topic, it must be underlined that studying popular fiction certainly does not indicate a 'dumbing down' or dilution of scholarly integrity, nor does it in any way undermine the high cultural status or value rightly afforded literary fiction. What it *does* do is require students and scholars to think seriously about the ways in which canons are constructed, to question the mechanisms by which texts are included or excluded from critical notice, and to consider the ways in which the world around us – and, just as importantly, our own sense of self – is informed by the narratives that we consume as readers and then absorb into our own imaginative and intellectual frameworks. Rather than reflecting a 'decline' in critical standards, the fact that serious attention is being paid to popular fiction, and to specific popular genres, is instead indicative of a continued growth in self-confidence and maturity for the discipline of literary studies.

As the terms and concepts outlined in the sections that follow indicate, popular fiction is an attractive and entirely valid subject of academic study not just because, as critics have often noted, it provides an invaluable insight into the passions, predilections and prejudices of the so-called 'ordinary' reader, but also because it has long been understood that, like mass culture more generally, these texts serve a significant ideological function. As such, they shape the world and our reactions to it, in ways we are only just beginning fully to comprehend.

There is much work still to be done. It has taken many years for popular fiction to make its way onto university reading lists, and even then it is still only within the past thirty years that major genres such as horror and the gothic, science fiction, fantasy and the romance have been academically investigated in any kind of detail or with any consistency. Indeed, some hugely important genres (most notably the romance) are very neglected, albeit in that instance with the exception of a handful of seminal publications. The transformation in popular reading habits, reception, production and distribution brought about by the Internet and social media is another area of urgent academic significance. Fanfiction and fan responses to popular texts are now increasingly the subject of fascinating and much-needed critical research, and it is likely that the related boom in self-publishing by both aspiring and established genre authors will soon attract even more deserved critical attention than has so far been the case. Furthermore, although there are clear historical reasons for the existing critical bias towards authors and texts from the UK and North America, there is also huge scope for popular fiction studies to engage much more fully with the work of writers who have emerged from national, racial and cultural contexts that have hitherto been overlooked or ignored in favour of overwhelmingly white, Anglophone and Western authors.

Key Concepts in Contemporary Popular Fiction is intended to serve as a reliable and concise starting point, rather than as an exhaustive or definitive analysis of the entire subject area, and so there are many considered exclusions and necessarily brief summaries of complex and much-debated concepts and terms in this volume. The bibliographies featured here therefore provide numerous suggestions for more advanced critical reading. The volume consists of five main sections. The first, and the most substantial, is the A–Z guide, which is intended to broaden significantly the critical vocabulary of anyone with an interest in contemporary popular fiction. Particular effort has been made to ensure that this section is as up-to-date as possible. Many entries related to recent developments in digital publishing, fanfiction and new and emerging genres and sub-genres have been included, and will be updated in future editions. Some of the terms listed here are in fact being defined in an academic reference work for the first time, and as such, it should be noted that widely accepted definitions of terms such as 'Cli-Fi', 'Bizarro Fiction' and 'Domestic Noir' are, at the time of writing, not yet fixed. I have instead tried to reflect the way in which these new and emerging terms are most commonly used at the present time.

The second major section is entitled Key Critical and Theoretical Approaches to Popular Fiction. Here, nine of the most significant and emerging theoretical approaches to the study of popular literature are briefly outlined. This section also serves as an introduction to the most important theoretical approaches to popular fiction. The roughly chronological arrangement of the section means that it provides a broad, summative overview of the evolution of academic and critical perspectives on popular fiction. The third section introduces six major popular genres – fantasy, crime, romance, science fiction, horror, the thriller and one major popular mode – the comic book/graphic novel. Each entry has a bibliography for those interested in knowing more about that particular genre. Then there is an annotated listing of fifteen of the most significant twenty-first-century popular fiction texts and, finally, a chronology of key dates which will help readers further pull together the critical and historical information they have gleaned from the rest of the volume.

Popular fiction studies is a rapidly evolving subject area, and it is for this reason that the eight key points listed earlier in this introduction should be considered as part of an evolving, rather than a fixed, framework for discussion. For instance, one of the most interesting developments within literary culture in recent years is what some commentators, particularly in US literary circles, see as the increasingly blurred lines between 'serious' and 'popular' fiction (it has also been called the 'Genrefication' debate, in response to critic Joshua Rothman's use of that term). This fascinating critical conversation reflects the fact that an award-winning literary novelist can now write an acclaimed zombie novel (Colson Whitehead's *Zone One* [2011]), or a fantasy novel (Kazuo Ishiguro's *The Buried Giant* [2015]), or a tale about the aftermath of a devastating pandemic in which a fictional graphic novel is of key thematic significance (*Station Eleven* by Emily St John Mandel [2014]). At the same time, genre writers such as Stephen King and Gillian Flynn now regularly receive fulsome reviews in the books pages, nominations for important literary prizes, and in King's case, prestigious medals.

It seems obvious then that the relationship between popular fiction and literary fiction is undergoing some radical and potentially far-reaching changes which must be acknowledged in this work (and have been), even if their full ramifications have yet to become clear. Just as academic definitions of popular fiction itself can never be entirely fixed, and have instead always developed in relation to specific historical, commercial and cultural factors, so too is it the case that the relationship between popular and literary fiction is always in a state of flux – and all the more so at this present time of huge commercial, technological and cultural change. It is my hope that the terms and concepts outlined here will provide not only a useful reference tool for students, academics and the general reader, but will also help spark further critical interest in this particularly exciting and worthwhile area of contemporary literary studies.

Bibliography

Berberich, Christina (ed.) (2015), 'Introduction: The Popular – Literature Versus *literature*', in *The Bloomsbury Introduction to Popular Fiction*, London: Bloomsbury, pp. 1–10.

Bloom, Clive (2008), *Bestsellers: Popular Fiction since 1990*, Basingstoke: Palgrave Macmillan.

Dalziel, Margaret (1957), *Popular Fiction 100 Years Ago: An Unexplored Tract of Literary History*, London: Cohen and West.

Gelder, Ken (2004), *Popular Fiction: The Logistics and Practices of a Literary Field*, London: Routledge.

Glover, David and Scott McCracken (eds) (2012), 'Introduction,' in *The Cambridge Companion to Popular Fiction*, Cambridge: Cambridge University Press, pp. 1–14.

Hoppenstand, Gary (2016), 'Genres and Formulas in Popular Literature', in G. Burns (ed.), *A Companion to Popular Culture*, Chichester: John Wiley and Sons, pp. 101–22.

McCracken, Scott (1998), *Pulp: Reading Popular Fiction*, Manchester: Manchester University Press.

Neuburg, Victor E. (1977), *Popular Literature: A History and Guide*, London: Penguin.

Pittard, Christopher (2015), 'The Victorian Context: Serialization, Circulation,

Genres', in C. Berberich (ed.), *The Bloomsbury Introduction to Popular Fiction*, London: Bloomsbury, pp. 11–29.

Williams, Raymond (1983), *Keywords: A Vocabulary of Culture and Society*, New York: Oxford University Press.

A–Z of Key Concepts and Terms

Acafan Term meaning 'academic fan' (sometimes rendered as 'aca-fan') which emerged during the 1980s as a means of denoting a scholar who engages in the study of fandom and self-identifies as a fan. The term was further popularised by Matt Hills in *Fan Cultures* (2002) and Henry Jenkins in his blog 'Confessions of an Aca Fan'.

'Aga Saga' Term used to describe a form of (usually) female-authored **popular fiction** particularly popular in the United Kingdom during the 1990s. According to Deborah Philips (2006), the sub-genre can be distinguished from other forms of romance fiction by its specific focus upon the domestic and romantic travails of middle-class, middle-aged women. The use of the term 'Aga Saga' is derived from the fact that in the UK the Aga stove has long been considered a marker of a certain type of cosy middle-class lifestyle. As Philips notes, the typical heroine is an overlooked middle-aged woman who has subordinated her own dreams to those of her children and husband (2006: 97).

Airport Novel Phrase used to describe the kind of supposedly unde-manding genre fiction purchased when one is in transit, and in need of fast-paced, accessible and escapist reading material. The 'airport novel' is therefore a Jet-Age successor to the 'railway fiction' of the late nineteenth and early twentieth-centuries. This kind of fiction is also seen as being briefly enthralling yet ulti-mately disposable. To describe a work of fiction as an 'airport novel' is therefore not always intended as flattery. In *Language in Popular Fiction* (1990), Walter Nash uses the setting of the airport lounge as a playful starting point for his consideration of style and gender in genre fiction.

Alternate History Also known as 'alternate world' or 'counterfac-tual' fiction (the latter is the term preferred by historians). As Karen Hellekson states, the core premise of any alternate history is the idea that a crucial event did not happen as we know it did (2001: 2). Many of the best-known alternate history novels involve imagining different outcomes for the Second World War. Foremost amongst these is Philip K. Dick's *The Man in the High Castle* (1965) and Robert Harris's 1992 bestseller *Fatherland*. Harry Turtledove is probably the leading contemporary exponent of the sub-genre, but other authors currently writing in this vein include Jo Walton (in her 'Small Change' series [2006–8]) and

Lavie Tidhar, whose novel *The Violent Century* (2013) features an alternate reality in which superheroes help change the course of the Second World War.

Amazon.com US-based online retailer that has done more than any other company to transform the publishing, distribution, marketing and reading of **popular fiction** in the twenty-first century. Founded in 1994 by Jeff Bezos, the company began operations as an online book retailer, but now sells products in almost every conceivable consumer category. Amazon first of all had a massive impact upon the fortunes of physical bookstores, with the profits of even large chain stores (such as Borders in the USA) eventually being massively undercut by the ease and perceived affordability of the company's vast online bookstore, selling both new releases and second-hand copies. Although there had been several previous attempts (most notably by Sony) to create an **e-reader** that would have truly mass-market appeal, it was only with the release of the first-generation Amazon **Kindle** e-reader in 2007 that the technology really took off with consumers (in large part thanks to the ease with which titles could be downloaded from Amazon's online store). More recently, Amazon has been a major force in the rise of self-publishing and digital publishing, with online platforms such as CreateSpace, **Kindle Direct** and **Kindle New Worlds** enabling aspiring authors to upload, format, market and sell their own fiction. Amazon also owns the influential online book-review/recommendation site **Goodreads**, the audio-book company Audible.com, and has its own publishing arm, with branded imprints related to all of the major popular genres, as well as a variety of other sub-genres and non-fiction categories.

Apocalyptic Fiction Apocalyptic fiction has long-standing history arguably going back as far as *The Book of Revelation*, in Western culture at least. One of the earliest bestsellers in colonial North America was a lengthy poem entitled *The Day of Doom* (1662), and US authors in particular have been exploring the theme with increasing variety ever since. The major means of bringing about the apocalypse have remained roughly the same for many centuries: they include the biblical apocalypse (see the *Left Behind* series [1995–2007]; cosmic catastrophe (as in Karen Thompson Walker's *The Age of Miracles* [2012] and Ben H. Winter's *The Last Policeman* series [2012]); the consequences of technological arrogance (which would include the many nuclear-related apocalyptic fictions as well as those relying on the ever-more popular 'artificial intelligence turns against us trope'); plague (a trend which began with Mary Shelley's *The Last Man* [1826] and continued in the likes of George R. Stewart's *Earth Abides* [1949], Richard Matheson's 1954 novel *I Am Legend*, and more recently, Emily St John Mandel's 2014 novel *Station Eleven*); and ecological catastrophe (as in Liz Jensen's *The Uninvited* [2012]). In the 1950s, Cold War, nuclear and technological anxieties brought about a boom in such texts on both sides of the Atlantic, such as Shirley Jackson's *The Sundial* (1956) and Nevil Shute's *On the Beach* (1957). The 1960s and 1970s saw the emergence of a spate of eco-catastrophe narratives, such as J. G. Ballard's *The Drowned World* (1962). The apocalypse is, of course, rarely the end in any of these texts: there are usually survivors, who try to rebuild civilisation, or slowly die in the ruins. As Kim Newman has noted, in reference to apocalyptic cinema, 'the more complicated a civilisation becomes, the more fun it is to imagine the whole works going up in flames' (1999: 18). Fictional representations of eco-crisis have taken on added urgency of late, as the devastating impact of climate change becomes ever more terrifyingly apparent (see also **Cli-Fi**). Thanks to the success of Max Brook's *World War Z* (2006) and the TV adaptation of Robert Kirkman's comic series *The Walking Dead* (2003–) zombie-centric catastrophes have also been very popular since the mid-2000s.

Audio Books Books recorded onto tape, CD, or, increasingly, digital downloads so that a narrative can be listened to rather than read, and now particularly associated with online companies such as Audible.com, Skybrite and Scribd. One of the first recorded novels (released on gramophone, and intended for the blind) was Agatha Christie's *The Murder of Roger Ackroyd* (1935). Now, every major fiction release is rapidly made available in digitally downloadable audio format. The format has been lent renewed popularity by the current ubiquity of portable audio devices. Increasingly, audio books are also being reconfigured so as to provide a more immersive experience. Some narratives are even being created for audio only, as is the case with Jeffrey Deaver's 2014 thriller *The Starling Project*, which was produced as a stand-alone example of 'audio entertainment' for Audible. com. Audio books are a major area of current growth for the publishing industry.

B

The **Bechdel Test** Created by American graphic novelist/memoirist Alison Bechdel, the 'Bechdel Test' has in recent years become a frequently cited means of drawing attention to the under-representation of female characters in popular culture. According to Bechdel's original 'test' – which took the form of a conversation in a 1985 issue of her comic *Dykes to Watch Out For* – there are three basic requirements that a narrative must fulfil in order to have 'passed'. 1. There have to be at least two women in it. 2. They have to talk to each other. 3. They have to talk to each other about something other than a man. Bechdel has said that she sees the test as being representative of her own career-long mission to represent women as subjects rather than objects. The Bechdel Test has now been succeeded by a number of supplementary 'tests' designed to highlight the under-representation of women and minority groups. These include the self-explanatory 'Racial Bechdel Test' and the 'Vito Russo Test', which relates to the representation of LGBTQ characters. Other recent variations include the 'Sexy Lamp Test' (proposed by comics writer Kelly Sue DeConnick): 'If you can remove a female character from your plot and replace her with a sexy lamp and your story still works, you're a hack' and the 'Mako Mori Test' (created in response to the 2013 film *Pacific Rim*), which relates to the degree of character and plot development afforded a female character within a given narrative.

Bestseller John Sutherland has defined the bestseller as 'commonly the book that everyone is reading now, or no-one is reading any more', thereby emphasising the ephemerality of such titles and their link to current popular taste (2007: 8). Clive Bloom anchors the term more directly in the commercial realm, characterising the bestseller as 'a book that enjoys phenomenal sales over a very short period of time', and noting that the term first entered the popular consciousness during the late nineteenth century, when the combination of cheap new printing technologies and the advent of mass literacy helped fuel the public appetite for **popular fiction** to an unprecedented extent (2008:1). These days, the term is generally understood to denote a book that achieves considerable commercial success and public prominence within a clearly defined period after publication (be it a matter of weeks after initial release or several months). In a subsequently often cited observation, sociologist Robert Escarpit distinguished between 'fast-sellers' that sell very well but only for a short period of time, 'steady sellers', which sell at a much more measured pace, but ultimately rack up very impressive sales numbers, and the 'bestseller', which combines the most lucrative qualities of both (1966: 118). The history of popular fiction is littered with poignant references to once immensely successful authors whose oeuvre has been forgotten by all but the most thorough scholars or avid genre enthusiasts. To be the author of a bestseller is no guarantee whatsoever of enduring literary fame.

As Ken Gelder observes, although many bestsellers can be classified as works of popular fiction, not all popular fiction titles will become bestsellers (2004: 3). More recently, John Helgarson, Sara Karrholm and Ann Steiner, the editors of *Hype: Bestsellers and Literary Culture* (2016) note that many bestsellers are acknowledged 'classics', i.e. works of 'literary' fiction. So it is important to remember that as several earlier critics have acknowledged, the 'bestseller' and the work of 'popular' fiction are by no means necessarily the same thing.

The modern conception of the bestseller is closely related to the establishment of newspaper bestseller lists, the most famous of which was started by *The New York Times* in 1931. Though it began as a listing compiled from the sales records of local booksellers, it quickly evolved into a nation-wide ranking system based on reports filed from all over the country, relying on data culled from book chains, independent retailers and wholesalers. Since 1984, the *NYT* list has been divided into fiction and non-fiction. The most significant recent change was the 2011 decision to incorporate data related to e-book sales. The paper also now has specific lists for children's fiction, non-fiction and graphic novels.

The concept of an official bestseller list was slower to take off in the UK, but since 1974, *The Sunday Times* has featured one, again compiled from weekly sales reports. Whilst some bestsellers do arise seemingly out of nowhere (here, the massive sales recorded by *Fifty Shades of Grey* [2011] even before it was snapped up by a major publisher comes to mind), many books of this nature have been granted a massive marketing push from their publishers, and novels written by certain authors are guaranteed a place on the list right away, due to their brand-name recognition and pre-release sales orders. The power of the 'official' best-seller list has always lain in its ability to perpetuate a feedback loop of higher visibility for the books featured there, first in bookstores (bestsellers and new releases that are *expected* to be bestsellers are usually prominently shelved) and now, increasingly, online.

Biofiction Term that refers to narratives that combine biographical elements taken from the life of a real-life figure (often a creative individual, such as a novelist, artist, or sculptor) with fictionalised components: see for instance two recent novels about specific episodes in the life of Henry James (*The Master* by Colm Tóibín and *Author, Author* by David Lodge, both 2004). John Sutherland also applies the term to popular narratives, as when he notes that Harold Robbins's *The Carpet Baggers* (1961) is a thinly disguised take on the life of Howard Hughes (2007: 68).

The Birmingham School Collective term for scholars and academics associated with the Centre for Contemporary Cultural Studies at the University of Birmingham, established by Richard Hoggart in 1964. Hoggart, author of the influential 1957 monograph *The Uses of Literacy: Aspects of Working Class Life* (one of the first major works of British cultural studies) also served as the centre's first director. Other important thinkers associated with the centre included Raymond Williams, Stuart Hall, Paddy Whannel and E. P. Thompson. As Daniel Horowitz observes, the centre 'came to exercise a commanding role in the field of Cultural Studies, shaping analysis of popular culture not only in Britain but also in the United States' (2012: 235).

Bizarro Fiction Bizarro fiction is characterised by its surreal, absurdist, grotesque and often comical stylistic and tonal excess. The sub-genre (an off-shoot of **weird fiction/fantasy**) has its origins in the output of a number of small presses specialising in cult fiction, amongst them Eraserhead Press, Raw Dog Screaming Press and Afterbirth Books. Bizarro fiction thrives on pushing plots and themes to their most absurdist and outlandishly grotesque conclusions, and many of the titles are notable for their deliberately eye-catching ridiculousness. These include *Help! A Bear is Eating Me* (2008) by Mykle Hansen; *Dungeons and Drag Queens* (2014) by M. P. Johnson; and the prolific Carlton Mellick's III's *Menstruating Mall* (2011), *The Morbidly Obese Ninja* (2011) and *As She Stabbed Me Gently in the Face* (2015). There are now websites devoted to Bizarro Fiction (such as bizarrocentral.com), short story collections, fan events and magazines.

Blockbuster The term 'blockbuster' was initially applied to cinema: the release of *Jaws* (1975) and *Star Wars* (1977) is often cited as marking the beginning of the blockbuster era. Within a literary context it refers to a work of **popular fiction** that has achieved an extremely high public profile and massive sales. As with blockbuster cinema, there is also an assumption that these titles are formulaic, fast-paced crowd-pleasers. Popular fiction blockbusters often feature attention-grabbing or taboo plot elements (i.e. sex and/or violence). The scandalous bestseller *Peyton Place* (Grace Metalious, 1956) and Jacqueline Susann's lurid 1966 **melodrama** *Valley of the Dolls* are often described as prototypical 'blockbusters'. Evan Brier notes that the term itself is 'an ambiguous product of the post-war emergence of mass culture' (2010: 114), whilst in 1981 Thomas Whiteside saw it as an indication of the then increasing trend amongst publishers to 'become focused on the pursuit of "the big book" – the so-called blockbuster' – in other words, a title that has deliberately been formulated to appeal to the widest audience possible, and has been supported by aggressive marketing and a well-promoted release date, as well as a barrage of related publicity (1981: 21–2). Citing the work of authors such as Arthur Hailey and Colleen McCullough, Scott McCracken has described the blockbuster as 'the defining popular genre of the 1980s' (2004: 620).

Bodice-Ripper A kind of romance novel, generally with a historical setting and explicit sexual content, so called because the covers often feature submissive young women lying in the grasp of a strapping (and frequently shirtless) suitor, whose ardour is so intense that he is literally ripping off her dress. The sub-genre, which was particularly prominent during the 1970s and 1980s, usually features a virginal heroine whose initial objections towards a handsome, charismatic but domineering older man are overcome by his animal magnetism and physical power. As such, they have often been accused in recent years of functioning as implicit or explicit rape fantasies (see Zidle 1999: 25). *Sweet Savage Love* (1974) by Rosemary Rogers is often held up as a prime example. More recently, it has frequently been suggested that E. L. James's *Fifty Shades of Grey* (2011) is essentially a contemporary take on the conventions of the traditional 'Bodice-Ripper'.

Bonnet-Ripper Romance sub-genre currently popular in the USA, particularly amongst Evangelical Christian readers. Many of the authors come from an Evangelical background themselves. The bonnet-ripper usually features a female protagonist who comes from an Amish or Mennonite background. *The Shunning* (1997) by Beverley Lewis is often cited as the first major example of the trend. During the course of these novels the protagonist usually embarks upon a forbidden but chaste romance with an 'outsider' that brings about a spiritual crisis. As Valerie Weaver-Zercher notes, this publishing category has become ever more popular in recent years, moving out from the Christian bookstores initially associated with the trend and into mainstream chains such as Barnes and Noble (2013: 7).

Book Clubs The most common current meaning of the term refers to an informal group comprised of friends or acquaintances that meets regularly in order to discuss a book selected as their subject of discussion. These kinds of gatherings have a long and distinguished history, and individual book clubs can focus on specific genres, non-fiction topics, current bestsellers or any other kind of volume. In recent years, the idea of the book club has experienced a major boom fuelled by the success of two high-profile television versions of the idea. These are: the 'Oprah's Book Club' segment of *The Oprah Winfrey Show*, which ran from 1996 to 2002 and, in the UK, 'The Richard & Judy Book Club', which ran on the *Richard & Judy* TV show between 2004 and 2009. Both clubs were regular segments on daytime television shows with largely female audiences.

Books selected for Winfrey's book club could automatically expect a huge boost in sales and public profile. Although many of the titles chosen were relatively recent publications (or new releases), even classic literary texts selected for the show became instant bestsellers. Ease of purchase was facilitated by prominent displays in many bookshops, and the fact that the books selected featured stickers emblazoned with the words 'Oprah's Book Club'. Not everyone was a fan: in 2002 Jonathan Franzen famously objected to the selection of his novel *The Corrections* (2001) on the grounds that he disagreed with the commodification of literary fiction he associated with the initiative. 'The Richard & Judy Book Club' imitated many of Winfrey's innovations and rapidly became very influential within the UK publishing industry. They tended to feature more genre titles than Winfrey, alternating them with literary fiction and non-fiction.

Though the show has now ended, the club still continues as a website operated in partnership with book retailer W. H. Smith.

The renewed popularity of the book club concept has led to a trend for special 'Book Club' editions of popular titles which feature 'bonus material' designed to foster group discussion. Book clubs are thriving in any number of places on the Internet. Facebook founder Mark Zuckerberg's resolution to read more books in 2015 led to the establishment of a 'Year of Books' Facebook discussion page which soon garnered more than 500,000 'likes'. Book clubs devoted to any and all genres, authors and topics can be found on the likes of Facebook, Twitter and Goodreads.

The term 'Book Club' can also be used to refer to the long-standing practice by which subscriber-based commercial companies send pre-selected books to their customers on a regular basis. Some of the most famous include 'The Book-of-the-Month-Club', Reader's Digest Condensed Books (now rebranded as 'Reader's Digest Select Editions') and the Library of America (which publishes beautifully designed hard-back editions of canonical American authors, although increasingly, genre authors have also featured).

Book Packaging The modern book-packaging industry emerged at the beginning of the twentieth century, when Edward Stratemeyer of the Stratemeyer Literary Syndicate began to 'market series (and book) concepts to publishers, then hire others to write stories to order, using specific titles, plot outlines and pseudonyms' (Johnson 2011: 308). Book packaging firms today also create series concepts and plot-outlines in-house and then commission writers to work according to the agreed outline, with the company retaining the legal rights and intellectual copyright to the resulting novel and the author receiving an agreed fee (often a small percentage of what the book will make in sales). The book-packaging industry in the US is dominated by Alloy Entertainment, which specialises in producing series for the **young adult** market. Their properties include *The Vampire Diaries*, *The 100* series and the *Gossip Girls* series. Other prominent book-packaging firms include James Frey's Full Fathom Five and Paper Lantern Lit, established by YA author Lauren Oliver.

The Booker Prize The Man Booker Prize (formerly The Booker Prize, and originally the Booker-McConnell Prize) was established in

1969 in order to recognise the best novel of the year written in English and published in the United Kingdom. It is now one of the most prestigious literary prizes in the world, and is awarded only to what the judges consider to be 'quality fiction'. A work of genre fiction has yet to be considered for the Booker, although the 2011 short-list was accused by some critics of being 'too readable', and in recent years, historically-based literary fiction by the likes of Peter Carey (*The True History of the Kelly Gang*, 2001 winner), Hilary Mantel (*Wolf Hall*, 2009 winner and *Bring up The Bodies*, 2012 winner) and Eleanor Catton (*The Luminaries*, 2013 winner) has often proved successful.

Bookwatch British company founded in 1982 in order to compile sales figures from bookshops and wholesalers so that they could be aggregated for *The Sunday Times* bestseller list.

Brand-Name Author A so-called 'brand-name author' is one whose work has become so well known and commercially successful that simply having their name on the cover of a new release is considered a powerful marketing tool. Indeed, on the covers of novels by brand-name authors, the author's name often appears in a larger font than the actual title. As John B. Thompson observes, if an author becomes a 'Brand Name' it is an indication that they have accumulated a substantial symbolic capital of their own, and can become more and more dependent on their own brand as opposed to that assigned to them by the publisher (2010: 215). Brand-name authors are almost always associated with one specific genre (even if, like horror author Stephen King or fantasy author J. K. Rowling, they also write in others), and as such, the purchaser of one of their novels can reasonably anticipate that buying it guarantees a particular kind of reading experience. Being alive is not a prerequisite for continued commercial success if one is a brand-name author, as the extensive publishing afterlives of J. R. R. Tolkien, Agatha Christie and Virginia Andrews (whose name continued to appear on ghost-writer penned novels for decades after her death) testify. Certain series also take on a brand-name status that transcends the lifespan of the original author, such as the James Bond series, the Sherlock Holmes stories and, more recently, Swedish author Stieg Larsson's *Millennium* series, which was continued by another writer after his death in 2004.

C

Canon The literary canon as it is traditionally conceived of is a list of set texts said to constitute, as Harold Bloom famously put it, the most 'authoritative in our culture' (1994: 1), although it is also a malleable and ever-evolving concept. The formation of a canon always has an ideological component, in that singling out any one text for particular critical notice always involves reflecting upon its perceived cultural, historical and social importance (or lack thereof, if it is excluded). As Trevor Ross notes, 'Today, canon-formation is almost exclusively associated with the mechanisms of cultural reproduction, and in particular with the establishment of university curriculum and syllabi' (1998: 10). Works classified as **popular fiction** have, in previous eras, almost always been excluded from the literary canon.

Category Fiction Term used (particularly within US publishing) to refer to genre fiction. Sometimes used in opposition to the term 'general fiction', which refers to titles that do not appear to fit into any one genre or genres. As a result general fiction is often used as a synonym for 'literary fiction'.

Celebrity Author Memoirs, novels and 'inspirational' or 'self-help' titles purportedly penned by celebrities have achieved particular prominence in recent years, with UK publishers in particular releasing a spate of such titles in the weeks leading up to Christmas holidays, in the assumption that they will be purchased as presents on the basis of name recognition alone. To be a celebrity author (as opposed to an author who has *become* a celebrity), one must have first achieved a degree of fame in an endeavour unrelated to writing (such as acting, comedy, music, or reality television). Although some celebrity authors do actually write fiction themselves, many of the novels released by celebrities are largely (if not entirely) written by professional ghost-writers, and, like supermodel Naomi Campbell's much-derided 1994 effort *Swan*, tend to feature plots which riff on some aspect of the celebrities' own persona. The British glamour model and reality TV star Katie Price has been particularly prolific in this regard. Memoirs penned by female comedians or comic actors have been big sellers in the US of late. Celebrity authors are also increasingly drawn from the online world. Beauty vlogger Zoe Sugg (aka Youtube star Zoella) released the novel *Girl Online* in 2014 and soon became the UK's quickest selling debut novelist.

Chick-Lit Term used to describe a sub-genre of **romance** fiction particularly popular during the mid-1990s and early 2000s. Chick-Lit generally focuses upon the loves and often humorous travails of urban professional women aged in their late twenties or early thirties. The watershed moment for the sub-genre is considered to be the publication of Helen Fielding's *Bridget Jones Diary* in 1996. The comic novel, which started life as a newspaper column in *The Independent*, had a distinctively self-deprecating heroine who, like many of her fictional successors, was on the one hand seemingly reaping the benefits of Second-Wave feminism's battles, yet has also found herself seized by the longing for a very traditional version of 'true love'. The typical Chick-Lit heroine works in an industry considered glamorous and exciting (PR, journalism, the fashion industry and show business all feature frequently. Sadly, academia does not). However, her impressive professional accomplishments are undercut by comic set-pieces and frequent social *faux pas*. Critical debates surrounding the sub-genre tend to revolve around the question of whether these novels represent an empowering take on popular post-feminist attitudes, or whether their frequent structural reliance upon conventional romantic resolution undermines any claim that these titles might have to be truly feminist.

Chick Noir Term used to describe the kinds of (usually) female-written psychological thrillers that have also been described as '**domestic noir**' and '**grip lit**', in which suspense arises from the treachery of familial and marital relationships, and the main character is almost always female.

Choose-Your-Own Adventure Choose-your-own-adventure series, usually targeted at children and younger teenagers, were particularly popular during the 1980s and 1990s. In these novels, the reader must make the choices that determine the outcome and development of the story. They could be considered an early and influential form of **interactive fiction**. In the USA, the R. A. Montgomery-authored Bantam Books series 'Choose Your Own Adventure' epitomised the format. It featured quest-driven narratives often belonging to the fantasy, mystery, or science fiction genres. In the UK, Steve Jackson and Ian Livingstone's *The Warlock of Firetop Mountain* (1982) launched the 'Fighting Fantasy' role-playing games series for Puffin, and resulted in many sequels, as well as role-playing board games and video games titles. Livingstone and Jackson also helped found the Games Workshop company, which spawned the *Warhammer* series of miniature war-games, as well as the 'Black Library' imprint, which publishes fiction set in the *Warhammer* universe.

Christian Fiction Christian fiction is defined by John Mort as fiction that focuses upon a conflict related to Christian principles (2002: 1). It is currently dominated in the US by fiction written by and for an Evangelical audience. Historical novels with a Biblical setting were very popular in the late-nineteenth and early-twentieth centuries. These included *Ben-Hur: A Novel of the Christ*, by Lew Wallace (1880); and *The Robe* by Lloyd C. Douglas (1942). Nowadays, Christian fiction can encompass any number of popular genres, but the most common include romance, inspirational fiction, historical fiction and supernatural horror. The most high-profile Christian fiction of recent decades has been the *Left Behind* series (1995–2007), written by Tim LaHaye and Jerry B. Jenkins, which now encompasses sixteen novels and has to date spawned two critically derided film adaptations, including a particularly poor 2015 version which provided further evidence of the sad decline of Nicolas Cage's once impressive acting career/hairline. *Left Behind* and its sequels dramatise the 'Tribulation' – the period following the 'Rapture' during which a disparate group of men and women 'left behind' on earth must battle to defeat the Antichrist (who is here, impressively, both the Secretary General of the United Nations and *People* magazine's 'Sexiest Man Alive'). The fast-paced, action-packed series helped establish Christian fiction as a mainstream publishing category in the US. Whilst the *Left Behind* series adhered to the tenets of the Dispensationalist branch of fundamentalist Christianity, other Christian fiction titles cater to the interests of readers from a broad range of denominations, sects and interest groups.

Class When considering **popular fiction** from a critical and historical perspective, social class – and in particular, the class of the assumed reader – has always been significant. From the earliest attempts to discuss popular fiction as a specific literary category, it has often been confidently asserted that a taste for such narratives is overwhelmingly associated with 'lower-class', 'working-class', or 'common' origins, despite the fact that, as Scott McCracken rightly observes, 'the social groups that make up the audience for popular fiction are diverse and overlapping' (1998: 5).

In 1957, Margaret Dalziel, like many critics to follow in her footsteps, rightly linked the rise of popular fiction to the mid-nineteenth-century advent of cheap periodicals (such as **penny dreadful**s) that reflected the tastes of an increasingly literate mass audience. Writing in 1977, Victor E. Neuburg described popular literature as 'what the unsophisticated reader has chosen for pleasure' and adds that while such a reader may come from any class, the primary appeal of popular fiction reading has been to the poor and to children (two groups often placed together by the arbiters of public taste) (1977: 12). It's a perspective also found in many of the earliest attempts to grapple with what we would now call 'popular culture'. Matthew Arnold's essays in *Culture and Anarchy* (1869) were in part inspired by concern regarding the supposedly disruptive nature of working-class entertainments, and by the belief that 'culture' had the potential to be an immensely important and positive influence upon the middle classes. F. R. Leavis argued in his 1930 essay on 'Mass Civilisation and Minority Culture' that only an educated and increasingly embattled elite could truly appreciate (and evaluate) art and literature, as did Q. D. Leavis in *Fiction and the Reading Public* (1932).

In what became an often replicated assumption, industrialisation and mass production were seen to have eroded the boundaries between 'high' and 'low' culture and created a kind of 'levelling down' effect, rendering the 'average' (which is often a synonym for 'working-class' or 'lower-middle-class') reader a much less 'cultivated' individual than they had been in the past. For **Frankfurt School** thinkers Theodor Adorno and Max Horkheimer 'mass culture' was a commercially codified means of pacifying and controlling the working classes, a form of 'anti-Enlightenment' that fettered consciousness and even had the potential to actively impede true democracy.

Indeed, the question of to what extent popular culture serves to help maintain the political and economic status quo, or has the potential to act as a liberating and even subversive impetus for change has long been a key preoccupation of critics concerned with class relationships in particular. **Cultural studies** in the UK (which significantly shaped the academic study of popular fiction as it exists today) essentially began with explorations of working-class popular culture by scholars such as Richard Hoggart, E. P. Thompson, Raymond Williams, Stuart Hall and

Paddy Whannel. Critics have also long been concerned about the effect that popular culture has upon the middle classes, and there exists a multitude of terms to describe the assumed middle-class reader and the material that is said to be targeted at them. Along with '**highbrow**' and '**lowbrow**', '**middlebrow**' emerged in the 1920s as a shorthand for a form of popular culture that occupied a half-way point between 'high' culture and 'low' or 'mass' culture. In 1960 American critic Dwight Macdonald coined the term '**midcult**' in order to describe works of art that paid lip service to the standards of high culture but in fact corrupted them. French sociologist Pierre Bourdieu analysed the way in which cultural taste proved to be a vital component of middle-class, 'bourgeois' identity in his landmark study *Distinction* (1977). More recently, critics of popular fiction have tended to move away somewhat from purely class-based discussions of popular narratives, in part because it is taken as a given that such texts attract readers from a broad social spectrum, and always have. This is certainly not to say, however, that we should downplay the obvious historical relationship between urban working-class culture in the eighteenth and nineteenth centuries and the emergence of popular genres in the first place, or ever discount the significance of social class entirely.

Cli-Fi Portmanteau term derived from the phrase 'Climate Change Fiction' usually said to have been coined by blogger and journalist Dan Bloom in 2007. Bloom used the term to describe novels that he considered to be 'Climate Fiction': i.e. a sub-genre of **science fiction** that takes as its major theme the immediate effects and wider ramifications of global warming. Bloom states that he intended the term to serve as a 'wake-up call' in order to underline the immediacy and urgency of the crisis. It wasn't until the term began to be used by major media outlets during 2012/13 to describe a new wave of fiction concerned with this subject matter that 'Cli-Fi' became widely used. There have even been suggestions that it represents a new genre in its own right. However, this claim has angered some science fiction critics, who rightly point out that the genre already has a long-standing history of producing novels focused on the devastating impact of climate change.

Comics see entry in Major Popular Genres section

Comic Fantasy Sub-genre of fantasy notable for the foregrounding of humour, whether in the form of knowing parodies or subversion of genre tropes, clichés and plot conventions. **Epic,** or 'high' fantasy, perhaps in part due to the sub-genre's occasional tendency towards pomposity, is a particularly common target, as with the likes of Piers Anthony's *Xanth* series (1977–) and Diana Wynne Jones's witty non-fiction 'guidebook' *The Tough Guide to Fantasyland* (1996) testify. Comic fantasy is also characterised by frequent comic set-pieces, puns and other word play, and a wry sense of genre self-awareness. Sometimes comic fantasy can take the form of novel-length parodies of specific series, as in the self-explanatory *Bored of the Rings* (1966), and sometimes the comic elements are woven into an elaborate fantasy world of that author's own creation, such as in Terry Pratchett's *Discworld* series (1983–2015), which with every instalment became ever more elaborate and intellectually ambitious. **Urban fantasy** novels often feature protagonists with a self-deprecating sense of humour, but tend not to rely on the comedic set-pieces, word play, or the kind of metafictional self-awareness that characterises comic fantasy.

Comic Strip Comic strips were a common feature of newspapers from the late nineteenth century up until the present day, but were particularly significant during the 1930s, when they contributed to the emergence of the comic book. Early comic strips to hit the big time included *The Katzenjammer Kids* (1897–), *Little Orphan Annie* (1924–2010), *Dick Tracy* (1931–), *Rupert the Bear* (1920–) and *Flash Gordon* (1934–). In the 1960s and after well-known titles included *Peanuts* (1950–2000), *Garfield* (1978–), *Doonesbury* (1970–) and *Calvin and Hobbes* (1985–1995). Comic strips were usually published in black and white during the week, with a larger-sized colour supplement at weekends. Although they have now been dropped by many daily newspapers (the money to be garnered from national syndication has been hard hit by the closure of many newspapers), comic strips are currently thriving online. Some of the most notable web-based titles include *Hark! A Vagrant* (which often parodies classic literary texts), *Penny Arcade*, *XKCD*, *Piled Higher and Deeper* (an uncannily accurate take on the unfortunate lot of the PhD student), *The Perry Bible Fellowship* and the surprisingly melancholy *Garfield Minus Garfield*, which reprints original Jim Davis strips with the eponymous feline erased entirely, 'in order to reveal the existential angst of a certain young Mr John Arbuckle'.

Covers When it comes to **popular fiction**, you can usually judge a book by its cover. Novels conforming to specific genre conventions almost always have covers that aid the reader in quickly selecting a title that suits their own particular reading interests: many books will even list the genre to which they belong on the spine or the back cover so as to further facilitate immediate identification by potential readers and categorisation by booksellers. **Chick-lit** novels often have covers with pink colouring, pictures of shoes, women's legs and shopping bags; **epic fantasy** titles feature a preponderance of dour-looking, sword-wielding men and women in hooded cloaks; military science-fiction titles usually have a uniformed protagonist wielding a weapon amidst the backdrop of a field of stars; and the success of *Fifty Shades of Grey* (2011) prompted the publication of numerous works of **erotic fiction** with copycat monochrome covers. The aim is to physically resemble a title that has already achieved proven commercial success, so as to hopefully encourage the would-be reader to purchase more of the same.

The current popularity of **e-readers** and tablets poses an interesting challenge for publishers in that such titles obviously do not have covers in the traditional sense of the word, prompting a 2012 article in *The Atlantic* to ask, 'Has Kindle Killed the Book Cover?' Online stores such as **Amazon** reduce the cover art to thumbnail size and e-book covers certainly do not have the same importance that they do for hard-copy versions of the text, which must attract attention in a physical rather than an online marketplace. Earlier versions of the **Kindle** also rendered images in black, white and grey only, and many e-books don't have a cover at all once downloaded. However, even when appended to e-books, it is still said to be the case that covers increase sales substantially. Many of the self-published authors making their work available as digital downloads do not have the support of professional artists and designers. As a result, there are now several websites devoted to unintentionally hilarious e-book covers created by amateur designers, including the oddly mesmerising Tumblr page 'Kindle Cover Disasters'.

Creepypasta The term originally derives from 'copypasta' (which referred to an excerpt of text copied and pasted from elsewhere on the Internet), and is now widely used to refer to horror, supernatural and paranormal-themed stories, photoshopped images, videos and audio files that originate on online user-generated forums such as Creepypasta.com. Creepypasta stories are often (but not always) told in a first-person confessional format designed to heighten immediacy and impact. They also often have a dramatic last-minute twist that underlines the format's debt to the oral urban legend tradition. As the FAQ section on Creepypasta.com (currently the most prominent site of this nature) makes clear, there are some selective criteria for publication, including a inclination towards stories that conform to the moderator's definition of 'creepy'; and a preference for narratives which involve the creation of an unsettling atmosphere rather than those elements it characterises as 'legitimately disturbing' (i.e. depictions of graphic physical or sexual violence). Stories are afforded prominence on the site according to how many readers 'up vote' or 'down vote' them. Readers can also leave comments and plot suggestions for the author and other users to read. Creepypasta.com was afflicted with brief tabloid notoriety in 2014 when it was linked to an attempted murder allegedly inspired by the controversial 'Slender Man' meme which actually originated in 2009 on another forum altogether, but was embraced by users of Creepypasta.com, who wrote countless stories inspired by the original concept and helped create an elaborate shared mythology.

Cthulhu Mythos Term coined by writer August Derleth that refers to the organising principle behind American horror/weird fiction author H. P. Lovecraft's best known stories. In tales such as 'The Call of Cthulhu' (1928), Lovecraft created an elaborate and remarkably bleak pseudo-mythology revolving around the idea that humankind exists in a vast and essentially hostile universe populated by immensely powerful and unfriendly extraterrestrial entities. Lovecraft's work was popular with a number of other **weird fiction** authors during the 1930s and 1940s, some of whom began to integrate references to it into their own work, and it wasn't long before the 'Lovecraftian' tale became a distinct form of weird fiction in its own right. Echoes of the 'cosmic horror' and existential angst found in the mythos can be detected in the likes of the crowd-sourced backstory to the 'Slender Man' meme, and the first season of the television series *True Detective* (2014).

Cultural Capital Term used by French sociologist Pierre Bourdieu to describe the social and economic benefits that are extended to the individual who attains a certain degree of cultural knowledge and competency within capitalist society. Cultural capital can be transmitted through the family, through education, and by means of one's wider social and institutional education. The concept is important to us here because in essence it suggests that our social class, educational background and material circumstances equip us with the tools which allow us to fully engage (or not) with a particular cultural artefact. As Bourdieu himself put it 'a work of art has meaning and interest only for someone who possesses the cultural competence, that is the code, into which it is encoded' (1999: 2).

Cult Fiction The term refers to fiction which has a niche but devoted following of readers who fiercely identify with the text. Thomas R. Whissen suggests it is 'a reader-created genre which depends on the reader having a very personal response to the text in question' (1992: xiii). The protagonists of cult texts will often be rebellious outsiders with an anti-establishment ethos. 'Cult' **popular fiction** tends to arise most consistently from within particular genres and sub-genres, most frequently science fiction, horror and fantasy (in particular, 'weird fiction'). However, Ana Sobral also argues that, 'Cults essentially reflect the tastes and opinions of a particular community of readers', and a 'cult' text can have either 'highbrow' or 'lowbrow' qualities (2012: 56).

Culture Industry Term formulated by **Frankfurt School** critics Theodor Adorno and Max Horkheimer in their essay 'The Culture Industry: Enlightenment as Mass Deception', published in *Dialectic of Enlightenment* (1944: published in revised form in 1947). They initially used the term 'mass culture', but removed it from later drafts because they wanted to exclude from the outset the suggestion it was a form of popular culture arising spontaneously from the people themselves, rather than something that was deliberately imposed from above by vested capitalistic interests (Adorno 2010: 98). The term refers to the manufacture of mass-produced, formulaic and pre-patterned cultural products (they were specifically referring to films, radio shows and magazines) which forever promise more than they can deliver, and are created in response to an entirely manufactured need. These products are said to frustrate genuine emotional catharsis in order to help subordinate the individual consumer's desires to the capitalist, profit-driven motives of the supplier. Adorno and Horkheimer argued that culture as it currently existed was characterised by a dismaying homogeneity because 'Films and radio no longer need to present themselves as art. The truth that they are nothing but business is made into an ideology to legitimize the trash they intentionally produce' (2002: 95). In his 1963 essay 'Culture Industry Reconsidered', Adorno further argued that the 'Culture Industry' 'transfers the profit motive naked on to cultural forms' (2010: 99), and forces together high and low culture, thereby snuffing out any potential for resistance within lower art in order to maintain social control (2010: 98). Adorno makes it clear here he did not intend their use of the word 'industry' to be taken literally; rather, the phrase refers to 'the standardisation of the thing itself – such as that of the Western, familiar to every movie-goer – and to the rationalisation of distribution techniques, but not strictly to the production process' (2010: 100).

Cultural Materialism Term associated in a Cultural Studies context with Raymond Williams, who defined it as 'a theory of the specifics of material culture and literary culture within historical materialism' (1977: 5). Cultural materialists read a work of **popular fiction** from a critical perspective that emphasises the importance of the historical, social, racial, gender and economic contexts of the text (though not necessarily all at the same time).

Cultural Studies In the UK, Cultural Studies as an area of academic inquiry was first established at the Centre for Contemporary Cultural Studies at the University of Birmingham in 1964 (also known as '**The Birmingham School**'). It is a fluid and interdisciplinary academic field drawing upon concepts and methodological approaches related to anthropology, sociology, psychology, politics, film studies and literary studies (Hartley 2003: 8). As John Storey notes, Raymond Williams's post-Marxist social definition of 'culture' broadens out the definition of the word beyond 'elite' texts and practices to encompass a much wider range of practices and events, and makes the study of culture and power, as well as the meanings and values implicit in 'a particular way of life' a central concern of his colleagues and successors (2009: 86).

Culture Wars Term which came to prominence in the US during the 1990s and which refers to a perceived conflict between liberal (i.e. socially progressive and left wing) values and conservative (right wing and socially 'traditionalist') values played out in the venue of culture. It was popularised by James Hunter (1992), who suggested that US society can be divided into two camps; 'the orthodox' and 'the progressive', each with notably different ways of perceiving the world, which results in clashes that play out in the media, law, politics and mass entertainment, and which particularly attach themselves to issues such as the abortion rights, gay marriage and affirmative action debates. The so-called '**sad puppies**' controversy surrounding what many considered to be a rigged ballot for the 2015 Hugo Awards (one of the most prestigious in science fiction) has been characterised as one of the most high-profile recent skirmishes of the on-going 'war' in a **popular fiction** context.

Cyberpunk Science Fiction sub-genre that reflects the growing significance of computer networks and the transformative potential of information technology. The 1984 publication of William Gibson's *Neuromancer* is usually cited as a key moment for the sub-genre, but the writers such as Bruce Sterling, Pat Cadigan, Rudy Rucker and, more recently, Neal Stephenson are also considered pivotal figures. Cyberpunk often features texts set in a near future dominated by powerful corporations, and frequently focuses upon the relationship between humanity and technology, as well as altered physical and mental states. In recent years, it has also become a frequent vehicle for the dramatisation of issues related to post-humanism and trans-humanism.

D

Dad-Lit Male-authored **popular fiction** narratives popular in the UK during the late 1990s and early 2000s which focused upon the emotional, romantic and domestic lives of fathers (or father figures, in the case of Nick Hornby's 1998 bestseller *About a Boy*), who are usually recently divorced, separated or widowed. The sub-genre is also associated with Tony Parsons and Mike Gayle. In the US, the term has of late been used to refer to self-deprecating non-fiction memoirs written by new fathers.

Derivative Work Term originating in copyright law which is of particular relevance to **fanfiction**. It refers to any creative work that is derived either partially or entirely from a pre-existing work.

Dieselpunk Emerging offshoot of **steampunk** which features deliberately anachronistic narratives set in an alternative version of the years between the end of the First World War and the beginnings of the 'atomic age' (the 1950s), with a focus on technology, weapons and visual aesthetics/costuming particularly associated with the rise of fascism, film noir and the inter-war period.

Dime Novels Sensationalist, cheaply produced and cheaply sold paperback novels particularly popular in the US during the period between the Civil War and the early twentieth century. Dime novels represent a precursor to the **mass-market paperback** genre fiction market. Their original price (ten cents) explains the name. As Edward T. le Blanc notes, whilst the earliest dime novels tended to feature distinctively American subjects – Westerns, biographies, historical fiction – a range of other genres soon became very popular, in particular adventure stories, romance and adventure tales (1996: 13).

Disaster Fiction Form of **popular fiction** that takes as its plot impetus some sort of devastating catastrophe, be it natural (earthquakes, volcanoes, storms), man made (climate change, devastating technological meltdown), ecological, or cosmic (meteor strikes, comets and the like). The disaster which serves as the focus of such a text may not be apocalyptic in nature (although it often is). Karsten Wind Meyhoff suggests that disaster fiction's typical setting is a large city, allowing for scenes of chaos in the street, and focuses on the choice facing an individual or a group of people who have survived the initial devastation in a time of great crisis, and always shows the before and after, with an emphasis on scenes of simulated destruction and mass death (2012: 304).

Disintermediation Term that refers to the reduction of importance now granted to the traditional gatekeepers between the consumer and the product that he or she wishes to buy (in this case, a work of **popular fiction**). Until relatively recently, if one wanted to purchase a novel, it was necessary to actually go to a bookshop, select the book and pay for it in person. Now, anyone with internet access can purchase a book in seconds, be it a hard copy for shipping or an e-book instantly downloaded to an **e-reader,** tablet or other mobile device. The current tendency towards disintermediation also extends to the creation, production and distribution of popular fiction. Authors no longer necessarily have to pass their work through the traditional chain of agents, editors, publicists and marketers. The internet has removed these 'barriers' due to the rise of electronic publishing platforms and the widespread availability of e-readers and e-reading aps such as **Kindle,** digital documents library **Scribd,** online bookstore iBooks, and the self-publishing platform **Wattpad.** The digital revolution has had a drastic (and for publishers and booksellers, often devastating) impact upon the production and distribution of popular fiction.

Domestic Noir Emerging publishing category associated with (mainly) female-authored psychological **thrillers** in which suspense and threat arises from conflicts and tensions associated with domesticity and intimate relationships, be they familial or marital. The term 'Domestic Noir' was first applied to this kind of fiction by the novelist Julia Crouch, who, in a 2013 blog post, described it as a **sub-genre** which 'takes place primarily in homes and workplaces, concerns itself largely (but not exclusively) with the female experience, is based around relationships and takes as its base a broadly feminist view that the domestic sphere is a challenging and sometimes dangerous prospect for its inhabitants'. As in Gillian Flynn's 2012 bestseller *Gone Girl*, the narrators of many of these novels are morally complex and unreliable individuals who relate stories of domestic abuse, marital unhappiness, emotional distress and dark secrets. The last characteristic frequently lends itself to the emergence of climactic twists that upend much of what we had previously believed to be true. As the 2013 publication of the anthology *Troubled Daughters, Twisted Wives* underlines, however, mid-twentieth-century American authors such as Dorothy B. Hughes, Elisabeth Sanxay Holding and Margaret Millar were already writing tense tales in what we would now call the 'domestic noir' vein long before the present-day resurgence of interest in the term. The terms **'chick noir'** and **'grip lit'** are also being used to describe novels of this type.

Drabble Work of short fiction intended to be no more than one hundred words long, although the term now more broadly can be applied to any work of fiction written with a very restrictive word count in mind.

Drugstore Paperbacks Term referring to the fact that in the US, **mass-market paperbacks** were often sold in wire racks placed at the front of pharmacies and grocery stores. Whilst cheap editions of classics and literary fiction also featured, the racks were dominated by popular genres such as **romance, crime, westerns** and **horror.** These volumes often had lurid covers that emphasised the suggestion that sex and violence were dramatised within (even repackaged works of 'classic' and 'literary' fiction were marketed in this way). Pocket Books, Avon, Fawcett and Penguin were the major players in this market.

Dystopian Fiction Sub-genre of **science fiction** that features a society (usually futuristic) which is in at least one significant respect considerably worse than our own. The protagonist is usually an oppressed individual whose desire for freedom and personal fulfilment is stifled by a brutal and repressive state. The struggle for liberty and happiness often drives the story, although many of the most famous classic dystopian narratives feature bleak or ambiguous endings that suggest that escape is ultimately impossible. It remains the sub-genre of science fiction most likely to be taken up by 'literary' authors, most likely because, like its flip-side, the utopian narrative (which imagines a world better than our own), dystopian fiction has always been a powerful means of exploring current philosophical, political and social anxieties. In recent years, dystopian **young adult** novels featuring teenagers who must reluctantly battle to overcome totalitarian regimes have become particularly popular, as have bleak visions of a near-future United States riven by plague, factionalism, ecological catastrophe and fascistic governments determined to erode female independence and reproductive rights.

E

E-books Books or documents that have been digitised and distributed as downloadable electronic files. The current popularity of the e-book format is directly related to the arrival of broadband internet and affordable, portable and user-friendly e-reading devices such as the **Kindle**, NOOK and Kobo (although these devices are now being superseded by e-reading apps downloaded onto tablet computers and smart phones). Although the concept of e-books has existed for many decades, earlier attempts to distribute books as computer files or on CDs, floppy discs, or tape, were stymied by a lack of convenience, portability and access. The release of the first-generation Amazon Kindle in 2007 sparked a renewed wave of consumer interest in the concept, and Christmas 2009 is generally cited as a tipping point for the e-book format, which became ever more widely adopted and accepted in the years that followed. Many e-books are actually scanned versions of hard-copy editions, but increasingly, **popular fiction** is being initially conceived of and distributed in e-book format. E-books commonly also include supplementary material. As a result, a book is no longer necessarily a physical object.

E-reader Hand-held electronic device upon which **e-books** are read. Although the likes of the Kobo, Nook, **Kindle** and Sony Reader were dedicated e-readers with limited or no internet access, the Kindle Fire, released in 2012, was also a multi-purpose tablet computer, and like the Tesco Hudl, reflected a shifting consumer preference for multi-function tablet devices. The 2014/15 fall in e-reader sales is in part a result of market saturation (e-readers are quite durable and long-lasting), and the fact that many people now prefer to read their e-books on tablets and smart phones.

Eco-Fiction Fiction that takes as its main subject and plot impetus environmental topics and themes: because climate change is a major preoccupation of contemporary eco-fiction, it has much in common with **Cli-Fi**.

Electronic Publishing Also known as digital or e-publishing: the term refers to the process by which **e-book**s are created, formatted, distributed and marketed.

Epic Fantasy Sub-genre of fantasy also often referred to as 'high' or 'heroic' fantasy. Novels and stories in this tradition tend to be heavily influenced by the work of J. R. R. Tolkien and the novelists who emerged in his wake, and are usually characterised by a vaguely medieval setting, quest-based narratives, the creation of elaborate secondary worlds, and background trappings such as armour, horses, limited technology and the use of swords and magic. Many recent epic fantasy narratives encompass multiple volumes, prequels, sequels and a large cast of characters.

Erotica/Erotic Fiction Form of **popular fiction** in which the narrative is organised around sexual set-pieces, and the unfolding of the physical/sensual relationship between the protagonists is the key narrative focal point. The current mainstream presence of erotic fiction (most **romance** publishers have specific imprints devoted to erotica) owes much to the arrival of the **e-reader**, which facilitates the instantaneous and anonymous purchase of material some readers might hesitate to buy in person in a bookstore.

Escapism The ability to fully 'lose oneself' in a book has always been cited as one of the greatest attractions (and dangers) of **popular fiction**. The purported ability (or inability) of a novel to help its readers 'escape' from their everyday lives and cares via the creation of a vividly realised imaginative world has long helped drive sales, and been posited as the reason why certain genres in particular (especially the **romance**) have such loyal audiences. The escapist potential of popular fiction also attracts suspicion from those who see this kind of immersion in a 'lowbrow' literary work as frivolous or even sinister. It is no coincidence then that metaphors related to drug-use and addiction are common even when fairly sympathetic commentators are talking about the appeal of genre fiction.

Excorporation Term associated with Cultural Studies scholar John Fiske, who characterises it as 'the process by which the subordinate make their own culture out of the resources and commodities provided by the dominant culture' (1989: 15). He cites the example of mass-produced jeans which are deliberately modified by their purchaser via the addition of bleach or strategically placed tears. **Fanfiction** could be considered an important form of literary excorporation, in that such authors are appropriating and personalising cultural products in inventive and imaginative ways not considered or sanctioned by the original creator.

F

Fairytale Literary genre with its origins in oral tradition, existing in almost every known culture, consisting of multiple tales told in hundreds of different versions, modified according to the teller, the audience and national or local context. Steven Jones Swann argues that while the fairytale, like the folk tale, often features ordinary people (as opposed to the gods who feature in myth), they differ from folk stories in that they also depict 'magical or marvellous events or phenomena as a valid part of human experience' (2013: 9). In **popular fiction**, cinema and television in recent years 'retellings' of well-known fairytales (and narratives which incorporate established fairytale conventions) have experienced a surge of popularity, with authors such as Naomi Novik, Neil Gaiman, Francesca Lia Block and Holly Black proving particularly adept at reconfiguring familiar tales for contemporary times. *Actual* fairies (or 'The Fae' as they are often characterised) regularly feature in **paranormal romance** and **urban fantasy** narratives.

Fake Lore Term coined by folklorist Richard Dorson in 1950, which he used to refer to deliberately manufactured/fabricated pseudo folklore masquerading as actual folklore (which organically arises from the people themselves), often for commercial or tour-ist-industry related ends. Of late the term has been frequently deployed by scholars discussing the emergence of influential horror memes on the internet, and in particular, the 'Slender Man' mythos.

Family Saga A work of **popular fiction** which traces the origins and fortunes of one family (or a number of connected families) over a matter of decades or even centuries. Often combined with romance and adventure sub-plots, and frequently featuring a historical setting (as in the work of British author Catherine Cookson), although elements of the family saga can surface in more spe-cific genre form, such as in the **gothic** fairytale 'Dollanganger' series, by V. C. Andrews (and later, her ghost-writer, Andrew Niederman) or the **science fiction** classic *Dune* (1965) by Frank Herbert.

Fanfiction Fanfiction is not-for-profit **derivative fiction** written by amateur authors. A work of fanfiction can be of any length, and is both penned and posted online by the fans of a specific pre-exist-ing fictional property, be it a novel or series of novels, television show, film, or cartoon (although thriving fanfiction communi-ties are also dedicated to the fictionalised exploits of real-life actors, singers, celebrities and pop groups). Fanfiction arguably has a history which long pre-dates the internet – the works of authors such as Arthur Conan Doyle, Jane Austen, Margaret Mitchell and Charlotte Bronte have all, for instance, inspired a wide range of prequels, sequels, **mash-ups** and retellings. Indeed, as Anne Elizabeth Jamison notes, 'fanfiction is an old story', but what is new is the current nature of 'writing's relationship to technology and the media' (2013: 17). The avid fandom that surrounded the television series *Star Trek* (1966–9) is often said to have spawned the fanfiction trend for 'Slash Fiction', in which characters, often same-sex, who would not have been romanti-cally or sexually involved in the source narrative, are paired up. The advent of online culture means that there exists a multitude of thriving sites dedicated to fanfiction. The most prominent at time of writing include Archive of Our Own, FanFiction.net and the self-publishing platform **WattPad**. Fanfiction emerges from collaborative communities and features a great deal of interac-tion between authors and readers. It is particularly associated with female readers and authors. Increasingly, certain fanfiction authors with big online followings are transitioning to mainstream publication; these include the likes of Cassandra Clare, E. L. James and Anna Todd, whose One Direction fanfiction series *After*, initially serialised on Wattpad, landed her a multi-book publishing deal.

Fandom Fan community that has attached itself to a particular work of **popular fiction** or popular culture, although the term is also used to refer to fan culture in the broadest sense of the word.

The Fantastic Term associated with Structuralist critic Tzvetan Todorov, for whom it is a form of literature defined by hesitation and narrative uncertainty. 'Once we choose one answer or another, we leave the fantastic for a neighbouring genre, the uncanny or the marvellous. The fantastic is that hesitation experienced by a person who knows only the laws of nature, confronting an apparently supernatural event' (1975: 25). Todorov's definition is a fairly broad one that can arguably be applied to many works of non-realist genre (and literary) fiction, in particular **horror**, the **gothic** and **weird fiction**.

Fantasy see entry in Major Popular Genres section

Fanzine Fan-created amateur publication devoted to articles, art and photographs related to a particular sub-culture or genre (i.e. punk music, cult or exploitation film, science fiction or horror fandom), individual characters or creators, or a specific text, such as a cult television show. Fanzines are always created and distributed by the fans themselves, and have a distinctively homemade aesthetic and a not-for- profit ethos. After their heyday in the 1970s and 1980s, fanzines have increasingly moved online.

Fast-Seller Term employed by Robert Escarpit (1966) to distinguish between what he categorised as three types of best-seller: the fast-seller sells a high number of copies in a short period of time, but sales often peak quickly; the steady-seller has unspectacular but consistently solid sales; whereas the **best-seller** combines the high volume sales of the former with the consistency of the latter.

Fiction Factory Commercial enterprise devoted to the rapid creation, writing and selling of **popular fiction** designed to sell quickly and appeal to a wide (and often juvenile) audience. One of the earliest and most successful examples was Erasmus Beadle's so-called 'writers factory', where authors were commissioned to churn out **dime novels** for the mass market as quickly as possible on an 'industrial' scale (Ramsey and Zabelle Derounian-Stodola 2008:

266). Then came the Stratemeyer Syndicate, which dominated commercial children's fiction in the US for decades, and had a large team of writers turning out titles (under house names) for enduring series such as the *Bobbsey Twins*, *The Hardy Boys* and *Nancy Drew*. More recently, controversial American author James Frey has been accused of setting up a modern day 'fiction factory' staffed by recent MFA graduates commissioned to write **young adult** fiction series such as the best-selling 'Lorien Legacies' novels.

Flash Fiction Short form fiction characterised by its extremely restricted word count: also known as 'micro fiction" and closely related to the **drabble**.

Forensic Detective Story Sub-genre of **crime** fiction (owing much to the work of Thomas Harris, Patricia Cornwell and Kathy Reichs) that revolves around a protagonist or protagonists whose job involves solving the crime (often a grisly murder) by collecting and analysing evidence from the crime scene, or the body itself. Coroners, blood spatter analysts, medical examiners and forensic anthropologists regularly feature. Narrative set-pieces involve autopsies, evidence collection and the revelations they inspire.

Formula A reliance upon formula is frequently cited as one of the characteristics that most distinguishes **popular fiction** from **literary fiction**; indeed, popular fiction is even sometimes referred to as 'formula fiction'. Popular texts invariably belong to a particular genre or combine elements of a number of genres, and follow a particular set of narrative conventions that conform to pre-existing reader expectations. John G. Cawelti characterises formula as 'a synthesis of cultural mythology with archetypal story pattern', and further suggests that 'Formulas are cultural products and in turn presumably have some sort of influence on culture because they become conventional ways of representing certain images, symbols, themes, and myths' (1976: 3, 20). Popular fiction's reliance upon formula has often provided grist for critics for whom genre fiction can be dismissed as clichéd, predictable and unoriginal. However, it is also the case that a great deal of reader pleasure arguably comes from seeing how formulaic elements within a particular work have been reconfigured or subverted.

G

Geek Culture 'Geek' is a formerly pejorative term commonly used in the US to refer to an individual who is perceived as intelligent but socially awkward, and interested in subjects such as mathematics, engineering and computer science, in addition to supposedly 'niche' non-realist popular genres. However, mainstream popular culture is now so dominated by forms of entertainment with their roots in these very genres and modes, that it has persuasively been posited that we are now in an era where 'Geek culture' – characterised by an open and unapologetic passion for the likes of videogames, fantasy, science fiction and superhero narratives – dominates the cultural landscape.

Genre Broadly speaking, the term 'genre' refers to the set of characteristics generally associated with the specific type of **popular fiction** being referred to. All works of popular fiction belong to a particular genre or – as is the case with the likes of **urban fantasy** or **weird fiction** – are **sub-genres** combining recognisable characteristics from a number of genres (indeed, popular fiction is often described as 'genre fiction'). Popular fiction's reliance upon classification by genre is one of its most significant characteristics. As Ken Gelder observes, 'the entire field of popular fiction is written for, marketed and consumed generically: it provides the primary logic for popular fiction's means of production, formal and industrial identification, and critical evaluation' (2004: 40). Popular fiction authors are generally associated with one specific genre or set of related genres. Although the basic outlines of the most significant popular genres were established by the middle of the twentieth century (if not before), it is also important to note, that as Scott McCracken remarks, 'genre boundaries are never absolutely fixed. Each new example of a particular genre may modify and change what is understood by the classification it comes under' (1998: 12). New genres or sub-genres may also arise as a result of particular commercial, historical or creative circumstances (see, for instance, **Cli-Fi**).

Genrefication The so-called 'genrefication' or 'genre debate' relates to the relationship between **popular fiction** and **literary fiction**, and has been of particular significance in US literary circles in recent years. The term was coined by *New Yorker* critic Joshua Rothman, who argued in a 6 November 2014 piece for the magazine that a 'process of genrefication is occurring'. The term refers to Rothman's assertion that the boundaries between popular fiction and literary fiction are being eroded by the increasing use of genre conventions and tropes by younger writers who are as influenced by popular fiction and popular culture as they are by the 'traditional' canon. The 'genrefication' debate is also a reflection of the fact that the inclusion of genre components in a narrative no longer leads to the automatic dismissal of a text by **'highbrow'** commentators and publication venues.

Ghost Writer Author who is commissioned to write (or to co-write) a book that will be publicly attributed to someone else. Ghost writing is particularly common when it comes to celebrity 'authored' memoirs, autobiographies and novels. Ghost writers are often established professional authors who specialise in particular kinds of publication – for instance, memoirs by musicians, or sports stars. Within a **popular fiction** context, ghost writers can also be contracted to write novels that will be published under the name of (or in collaboration with) established genre authors. Thriller writer James Patterson has, for instance, always been very open about his frequent use of ghost writers, a tactic which ensures that the Patterson 'brand' always produces multiple new titles a year.

Goodreads Social media website which hosts and collates user-generated book recommendations and reviews. Members can create individualised 'virtual bookshelves' that allow them to list, rate and review books they have read or about to read. Members can also see the 'bookshelves' of other users, and receive personalised recommendations. The site was launched in 2007 and as of 2016 claims to have around 40 million users. It has become an important marketing tool for writers and publishers. The company was purchased by **Amazon** in 2013.

Google Books Digital library created by Google.inc which has the stated aim of digitally scanning every book in the world. Google Books quickly established partnerships with prominent university libraries which allowed their collections to be digitised, and many academic publishers and commercial publishers followed suit. When accessing a title in Google Books, a user can view the entire book (if it is out of copyright), have access to a select number of pages (which publishers hope will make the user more likely to buy the complete title via imbedded links to online booksellers) or see a 'snippet' of the text concerned. The initiative has proved controversial with some authors, and indeed, Google was sued for copyright infringement in the US by the Authors Guild. However, in October 2015, a Federal court ruled that Google Books' display of excerpts from copyrighted texts was legally acceptable under existing 'fair use' conventions.

Gothic Originally a vaguely pejorative term meaning vulgar, barbarous and old-fashioned (derived from the name of the Germanic tribes who sacked ancient Rome), the gothic is a genre that thrives on repression, concealment and terror. The gothic emerged as a distinct publishing category in 1764 with the publication of Horace Walpole's novel *The Castle of Otranto*, which provided an oft-imitated blueprint. The new genre received a further jolt of popularity in the 1790s in the wake of the upheaval caused by the French Revolution. The 'classical' European gothic novels tended to feature imperilled young heroines, sinister patriarchs, aristocratic protagonists and a continental European setting. A strong suspicion of Catholicism and 'foreigners' saturated the work of English authors in particular. The presence of the supernatural (or of supposedly supernatural elements which would later be revealed as sinister chicanery) was another stock trope. The gothic underwent a major configuration once it migrated to the very different political, religious and geographical landscapes of North America, and quickly became a key component in the establishment of an independent and distinctively American literary tradition. Anxieties about race, genocide, slavery, the hidden costs of stolen land and the seemingly vast and terrifying wilderness came to the fore. Distinct regional variations – such as the Southern gothic, the New England gothic, and the Midwestern gothic – later emerged. In recent years, Gothic Studies has become a particularly vibrant area of literary scholarship, and scholars are beginning to explore gothic traditions from a much wider range of national and regional contexts than ever before. An ever-increasing number of sub-genres related to the rapidly shifting contexts of contemporary life have been also identified, amongst them the eco-gothic, the biomedical gothic, the suburban gothic and the cyber gothic.

Gothic Romance (aka the 'Modern Gothic') The gothic romance sub-genre (which actually has little to do with the gothic as defined above) was particularly popular during the late 1960s and 1970s, and helped establish the mass-market romance as a major moneymaking concern for publishers. In the gothic romance, a chaste heroine is alternately menaced and wooed by a potentially threatening but charismatic older man with a terrible secret in his past. Both *Jane Eyre* (1847) and *Rebecca* (1938) are usually cited as major influences. The sub-genre's popularity inspired feminist critic Joanna Russ to write her classic 1973 article 'Somebody's Trying to Kill Me and I Think It's my Husband: The Modern Gothic', in which she classified them as 'neither love stories, nor stories of women-as-victims. *They are adventure stories with passive protagonists*' (1995: 111). The novels were usually sold in drugstores and supermarkets.

Graphic Novel see entry in Major Popular Genres section

Grimdark Recently emerged sub-genre of heroic/epic fantasy that has themes of an 'adult' and self-consciously gritty nature. Although the vaguely medieval setting, swords and armoured warriors often found in these texts recall the trappings of conventional heroic/epic fantasy, grimdark texts are notable for their cynical, bleak worldview, graphic depictions of sex and violence, and 'mature' take on traditional fantasy themes and tropes. Morally compromised anti-heroes often feature as the main protagonists, and the lines between good and evil are usually blurred beyond recognition. The sub-genre is associated with authors such as George R. R. Martin, Mark Lawrence and Joe Abercrombie.

'Grip Lit' Alternative descriptor for the post-2012 trend involving female focused (and often, female written) psychological thrillers (many of which have also been labelled as **'domestic noir'**). The term is said to have been coined in 2015 by the Irish novelist Marian Keyes, who used it to describe her fondness for 'really gripping books' about 'very recognisable women who live messy lives'.

Guilty Pleasures Term implying that **popular fiction** is a form of immersive entertainment readers consume with a certain embarrassment born of their awareness of its inherently frivolous nature. For instance, in a much circulated 2012 piece on genre fiction written for *The New Yorker*, Arthur Krystal characterised the novelistic 'Guilty Pleasure' as something we enjoy reading but are not proud of having consumed, once again deploying the addiction metaphor that so often comes in criticism related to popular fiction: 'A fix in the form of a story, a narrative cocktail that helps us temporarily forget the narratives of our own humdrum lives. And, for not a few readers, there's the additional kick of feeling like they're getting away with something.' As the current mainstream popularity of erotica amongst female readers in particular suggests, the advent of e-books has greatly facilitated the purchase and consumption of novels of this nature, although a 'guilty pleasure' can belong to any genre.

H

Habitus Term associated with Pierre Bourdieu. Our individual habitus are said to be the 'schemes of perception and appreciation' that shape our perceptions of the world and equip us to interact with the social structures and cultural products which surround us (1993: 64). Our habitus is informed by our familial and institutional education, as well as our social class. It is not necessarily fixed for life, in that new experiences and circumstances can alter our individual preferences and prejudices. The concept is related to Bourdieu's exploration of the reasons why different social classes develop markedly different cultural tastes.

Hardback Print edition of a novel that initially appears in a more expensive, hard-backed edition. Although many works of **popular fiction** first appear in paperback or trade paperback editions, hardback releases are often arranged for authors who have a reliable following of readers who will rush to buy their latest tome. Hardbacks will also appear from debut authors whose work has built up a great deal of pre-publication buzz. Rising **e-book** sales has meant that there has recently emerged a trend for releasing more attractive, limited edition hardbacks designed to attract collectors, the rationale being that consumers used to instantly downloading a cheaper digital version of the text will be tempted by a more collectible hardcopy.

'Hard-Boiled' Detective Fiction Variety of American detective fiction that emerged during the 1920s, having first arisen in pulp magazines such as *Black Mask*, where stories by Dashiell Hammett and Raymond Chandler first established many of the **sub-genre**s most salient characteristics. The typical 'hard-boiled' protagonist was a tough, cynical loner, usually a dogged private investigator negotiating 'a violent and corrupt urban terrain' (Horsley 2010: 32).

Harlequin This Canadian-based firm is the leading publisher of **romance** fiction in the world, and has been for decades. Harlequin was founded in 1949 in order to reprint cheap paperbacks for the mass-market audience. By the end of the 1950s, the company had acquired the North American distribution rights to novels produced by the British romance publisher Mills and Boons. They bought the firm outright in 1971. Harlequin, currently owned by Harper Collins, now has multiple imprints designed to appeal to almost every conceivable customer demographic and generic variation of the romance novel. They also publish books in a range of languages.

Highbrow Term used to describe a cultural product (or an individual) which/who is perceived as intellectual, serious and challenging. The term derives from the obviously erroneous belief that more intelligent individuals have physically larger brains, and therefore 'higher' brows.

Historical Romance Work of **romance** fiction with a historical setting. Popular sub-categories include Regency, Victorian, Tudor, Medieval, Pioneer, 'Pirate' and Viking romances.

Homogenisation In a **popular fiction** context, the term refers to the idea that the mass-produced and inherently formulaic nature of genre fiction (as well as the tendency of popular writers to seek to imitate past successes) means that the texts that result are repetitive, predictable and familiar. Adorno and Horkheimer decried what they viewed as the dismayingly standardised and numbing effects of popular culture produced by what they called the **'culture industry'**. In 1960, American critic Dwight Macdonald railed against what he saw as the homogenising effects of so called **'masscult'**, which supposedly destroyed value judgements, dissolved old barriers of class, tradition and taste, and 'scrambles everything together, producing what might be called homogenised culture' (2011: 11).

Horror see entry in Major Popular Genres section

Hybridisation In literary criticism more generally, hybridity is associated with post-colonial theory, but in a **popular fiction** context, it refers to the suggestion that popular genres are increasingly becoming more and more cross-fertilised, as tropes, themes and character types traditionally associated with one genre turn up in a text associated with another.

I

Imprint Specific brand within a publishing company which specialises in marketing and publishing novels associated with a particular popular genre or sub-genre. All major publishing companies have imprints. **Amazon** Publishing, at the time of writing, has fourteen imprints spanning a broad range of genres. So too does Hachette, whose most prominent imprints include the Orbit science fiction and fantasy line. **Romance** publisher **Harlequin** has imprints related to a wide range of sub-genres and categories within that broader generic designation. Imprints will usually have distinctive cover branding and their own logo in order to aid rapid identification by potential readers.

Incorporation Term coined by Cultural Studies scholar John Fiske related to his concept of 'excorporation'. It refers to the means by which the dominant system neutralises signs of resistance towards the dominant system by assimilating them into its own business model (Fiske gives the example of companies like Levi's producing pre-ripped jeans in order to satisfy consumers who might otherwise have altered the product themselves [2010: 13]). Within a **popular fiction** context, **Amazon**'s creation of the 'Kindle Worlds' imprint, which attempts to make money from officially licenced works of **fanfiction**, could be seen as a classic attempt at incorporation.

Interactive Fiction The term initially referred to text-driven computer games popular in the 1980s and early 1990s, in which the user decided their own fate by choosing whether or not to follow directive onscreen prompts. Key early examples included *Adventureland* (1978) and *Zork* (1977) but as computer processing capacities improved, graphics and gameplay became much more sophisticated, and these kinds of games ever more complex. Interactive fiction of this type remains popular with enthusiasts whose interest in the narrative possibilities of the format have been greatly facilitated by online culture, and by the creation of digital game-creation tools such as Twine, 'an open source tool for telling interactive, non-linear, stories'. It likely that **e-books** will continue to become more and more interactive in nature. Hyperlinks, video clips and animated graphics can all potentially be added to the textual apparatus of a digital text with relative ease.

K

Kindle Direct Publishing Online, free-to-use self-publishing platform established by **Amazon** which enables **e-book** authors to upload their fictional creations to Amazon's online bookstore, which will then host and sell the text for a cut of the proceeds. The platform represents a major form of disintermediation in that it actively encourages authors to bypass the traditional publishing gatekeepers. This also means that authors have to copy edit, format, design and market their own book (or pay someone else to do so). Authors can decide which level of royalty they will receive if any and when any copies are sold: at present they can be up to 70 per cent. They also retain the copyright to their own work.

Kindle Serials E-books made available for download in a number of episodic, regular instalments. Once a customer has paid for the first instalment through **Amazon**, the rest are free and will download automatically to their e-reader or tablet.

Kindle Singles E-book imprint owned by **Amazon** which specialises in books of all kinds – be they fiction, non fiction, or memoir – of between 5,000 and 30,000 words in length. Texts must be original, self contained and not have been previously published.

Kindle Worlds Self-publishing platform hosted and devised by **Amazon** that seeks to monetise and licence **fanfiction**. Would-be authors choose a specific, officially licensed 'World' (by which they mean an existing novel series, comic, film, or television show) and once they have written a story that conforms to the standards laid out by the rights holder, they can upload and sell their work on the Kindle World's e-publishing platform. Kindle Worlds has been controversial with pre-existing fanfiction sites and authors because the platform involves making commercial profit from what had previously been a resolutely non-profit amateur endeavour. A previous high-profile attempt to monetise fanfiction, the for-profit archive FanLib (2007–8) was unsuccessful.

L

Lad Lit Term used during the 1990s to refer to the work of British authors such as Nick Hornby and Mike Gayle who were associated with humorous novels about the lives and loves of single men in their late 20s and early 30s. 'Lad Lit' was sometimes posited as the male equivalent of **chick-lit** although it never achieved the same cultural prominence.

Leavisite Term used to refer to critics or commentators who take a perspective on literature and popular culture influenced by the work of F. R. and Q. D. Leavis.

Legal Thriller Legal thrillers feature a protagonist who works in the legal profession and finds themselves wrapped up in a complex and morally compromising case. The **sub-genre** is associated with writers such as Steve Martini, Brad Meltzer and in particular, John Grisham.

Liberal Humanism An essentially idealistic, romanticised approach to literary criticism informed by the belief that, as Matthew Arnold put it, culture should be 'the best that has been thought and said in the world', and as such, a defence against the indignities and cruelties of the modern world (2006: 5). 'Culture' in this sense of the word always means 'high culture'. The liberal humanist approach played a key part in the development and acceptance of literature as a valid topic for academic study.

Libraries Libraries have been immensely important in the development of **popular fiction**, because they provide those without the means to purchase books for themselves with access to a wide range of texts. Library lending records have also long been an important means of gaining a sense of popular reading habits. As Ken Gelder notes, popular fiction 'gained its broader circulation during the twentieth century precisely through its association with lending and commercial libraries' (2004: 78).

Light Novels Form of fiction popular in Japan. Light novels are designed to be readable, accessible, shorter genre novels aimed at a predominately **young adult** audience. They are written in a simplified form of Japanese alphabet in order to facilitate accessibility and readability. They are often related to Anime tie-ins and usually feature illustrations.

Literacy It was the emergence of a truly 'mass' audience that gave rise to **popular fiction** as we understand it today, in that it created the wider public appetite for accessible, sensationalist and entertaining reading material. In Margaret Dalziel's important early academic investigation of Victorian popular fiction, the mid-1840s is cited as the period when the mass production of fiction which even the poorest citizen could buy began (1957: 4), although as Victor Neuburg (1977) would later note, there was already a mass reading public in Britain by the end of the eighteenth century. Clive Bloom also stresses the pivotal role that literacy played in the development and origins of popular fiction, and referring to the late-Victorian era in particular, writes of the way in which 'the vast new pool of readers created by elementary education produced a huge new market for literary entertainment and printed information' (2008: 32).

Literary Fiction The relationship between 'literary fiction' and popular fiction has always been complicated. For critics such as F. R. and Q. D. Leavis, there was a clear and compelling distinction between 'good', artistic, challenging works of literary fiction (which could only be properly valued and appreciated by an elite but unappreciated minority) and the standardised, degraded and *degrading* cultural products of the post-industrial age, a line of thought that would be reflected to some extent in critiques of mass culture undertaken by the likes of Adorno and Horkheimer and Dwight Macdonald. Marc Angenot (1975) argued that popular/genre fiction was a form of **paraliterature** existing outside of the parameters of literary fiction which also provided a means for literary fiction to define itself as what it is not, a definition which was expanded upon by Christopher Pawling (1984: 2).

Leslie Fielder, fundamentally objecting to the idea of a divide between 'high' and 'low', suggested that the idea of a specific category of 'popular fiction' was the invention of 'certain theorizers after the fact. It exists generically in the perception of elitist critics [. . .] it will, therefore, cease to exist as a category when we cease to regard it in the way we have been misled into doing' (1969: 30). More recently, Ken Gelder has argued at length that popular fiction is 'best conceived of as the opposite of Literature (to which I shall ascribe a capital L, distinguishing it from literature as a field of writing). The reverse is also true, and in fact, it can often seem as if Literature and popular fiction exist in a constant state of mutual repulsion or repudiation' (2004: 11). Gelder argues that as a result, popular fiction is best considered on its own terms, a point anticipated by Tzvetan Todorov in his essay 'The Typology of Detective Fiction' (1977), when he argued that, 'as a rule, the literary masterpiece does not enter any genre save perhaps its own, but the masterpiece of popular literature is precisely the book which best fits its genre' and further comments that 'the same measurements do not apply to "high" art and "popular" art' (1977: 43, 44). In recent years it has also been suggested that the perceived boundaries between 'literary fiction' and 'popular fiction' are becoming increasingly blurred, as contemporary American writers in particular frequently make use of plots, themes and character types more usually associated with genre fiction (see also **genrefication**). However, there has also long been a general recognition that that which we define as 'popular' does indeed have some specific characteristics which are less pronounced in literary fiction (such as a reliance on formula, categorisation by genre and **sub-genre**s, and a tendency to be more visibly shaped by commercial and technological considerations), and there is also the fact that having some sense of these characteristics makes the academic study of the subject a more clearly defined endeavour.

Literary Guild American Book Club, founded in 1927, which is still in existence. The guild is run on a subscription basis: customers pay a set monthly fee and are sent a pre-selected number of newly published books by mail order, a list which often features pre-selected genre titles.

Lowbrow Form of **popular fiction** is supposedly unchallenging, unintellectual and formulaic, in contrast to challenging and artistic works of **highbrow** significance. A person can also be 'lowbrow' themselves. In an influential 1915 essay, Van Wyck Brooks claimed that American culture had been divided into 'highbrow' and 'lowbrow' camps since the days of Puritan intellectual Jonathan Edwards (who epitomised the former) and Benjamin Franklin (the latter) (Jumonville 2007: 205).

M

Magazines Magazines specialising (partially or wholly) in **popular fiction** were for generations a key means of distributing and sharing these kinds of narratives, from proto-magazines such as the **penny dreadful**s and penny periodicals that began to appear in the 1830s and 1840s to more respectable publications such as *The Strand Magazine*, *Blackwood's Magazine* and *Household Worlds*. Pulp magazines also helped shape the US **dime novel** market of the late nineteenth century. *Amazing Science Fiction* and *Astounding* both had a great deal of influence upon the development of the so-called 'Golden Age' of American science fiction in the 1920s and after, whilst *New Worlds* did the same for the British incarnation of the genre, and was later central to the ambitious and experimental 'New Wave' of British SF from the 1960s. *Black Mask* was pivotal to the establishment of **hard-boiled detective fiction**. Authors published in *Weird Tales* helped shape **horror**, **fantasy** and **weird fiction** to an immeasurable extent. Though they no longer wield quite the same power that they once did, several of the most notable genre magazines persist, as do a wide range of print and online small press speciality magazines such as *Cemetery Dance* (horror) and *Albedo One* (science fiction) as well as titles devoted to specific **sub-genres** (such as **grimdark** and **bizarro** fiction). During the mid-twentieth century, mainstream magazines such as *Playboy* and *Esquire* regularly published genre fiction. In addition, the history of what Nicholas Daly has characterised as 'Popular Modernism' is intrinsically linked to the thriving magazine industry of the 1920s and 1930s.

Manga Japanese comic book usually sold in digest format, wide range of popular genres and specific **sub-genres** unique to manga, such as *Shōnen* (boy's manga), *Shojo Manga* (girl's manga) and *Yaoi* (boy's love – magazines aimed at a predominately female audience that focus on romantic/homosocial relationships between young men). Even when translated into other languages, manga books are still read from right to left, and have a distinctive visual style that tends to privilege image over plot. The modern manga industry's emergence is often linked to the success of Osamu Tezuka, creator of *Astro Boy* (original run 1952–68).

Mash-Up Term originally deployed in relation to dance music to refer to the process by which two (or more) previously existing songs are combined to create a new, hybrid track. The term came to be used to describe the post-2009 trend for rewriting classic literary novels in order to incorporate genre elements. The originating text is Seth Grahame-Smith's *Pride and Prejudice and Zombies* (2009) which retains much of Austen's original prose and plot but transforms Elizabeth Bennet and her sisters into zombie-battling warriors (although in this case, the undead are known as 'Dreadfuls'). The success of this satirical take on Austen spawned a host of similar experiments, many of them also published by Grahame-Smith's publisher Quirk Books. A number of nineteenth-century classics were subsequently rewritten in order to incorporate, variously, vampires (*Jane Slayre*, 2010), love interests of a lupine nature (*Little Women and Werewolves*, 2010) and even robots (*Android Karenina*, 2010). Real-life historical figures such as Abraham Lincoln, Queen Victoria and, more recently, suspected axe-murderer Lizzy Borden (Cherie Priest's *Maplecroft*, 2014) have also transformed into defenders against all manner of supernaturally inspired threat, although technically these efforts are not mash-ups, because their prose and plots are original and not derived from an existing 'classic' literary property.

Mass-Market Paperback Term used in the US publishing industry to refer to cheap, widely available and attractively packaged paperbacks designed to attract as wide an audience as possible. The company usually credited with pioneering the format is Pocket Books, which was founded in 1939 in order to sell affordable reprints of bestselling hardback volumes. During the post-war era, companies such as Dell, Fawcett and Bantam emerged, all of them, like Pocket, specialising in cheaply produced, affordable fiction sold in drug stores, airports, supermarkets and grocery stores. Although many 'classic' works of **literary fiction** were also reprinted, the mass-market paperback industry was from the start dominated by works of genre fiction. That trend accelerated when Pocket started to commission their own 'paperback originals' which would bypass the hardcover stage entirely. According to John B. Thompson, the market for mass-market paperbacks began to reduce in the 1980s and 1990s because a more affluent readership was willing to buy hardcovers (which had themselves become more affordable) and trade paperbacks (2010: 39).

Mass Culture According to Richard Hoggart in *The Uses of Literacy* (1957), a new 'mass culture' was replacing the crude but genuinely 'of the people' kind of authentic urban working-class culture that he associated with his childhood (1957: 24). The 'new style of popular publications' Hoggart critiqued was said to be problematic not because the works failed to be **'highbrow'** (1957: 24), but because they were ultimately 'full of a corrupt brightness, of improper appeals and moral evasions' (1957: 340). Indeed, 'These publications do not contribute to a sounder popular art but discourage it [. . .] it is easier to kill the old roots than to replace them with anything comparable' (1957: 139). As in the earlier formulations of Adorno and Horkheimer, mass culture is here seen as being imposed from above, unlike 'folk culture', which is said to arise organically from the people themselves. Adorno and Horkheimer's term the **'culture industry'** is closely related, as is the term **'masscult'**. The products of 'mass culture' are generally perceived to be mass-produced, standardised and essentially inauthentic.

Masscult Term coined by Dwight Macdonald, who, in an influential 1960 essay for the *Partisan Review* entitled 'Masscult and

Midcult', argued that culture in the West was divided between 'high' or traditional culture, and 'a novel kind that is manufactured for the market' which he dubbed 'masscult' (2011: 3). Macdonald characterised it as 'a parody of high culture' that wasn't really culture at all. He argued that 'masscult' constituted the vast majority of new media, including radio, television and movies. In a position that owed much to the **Frankfurt School**, Macdonald claimed that masscult was a homogenised, standardised form of **middlebrow**, bourgeois cultural product 'fabricated by technicians hired by businessmen', which failed to provide the genuine emotional catharsis and aesthetic satisfaction offered by high culture, and granted only distraction and stimulation, but nothing more substantial (2011: 13).

The Masses Term often used to describe the great mass of 'ordinary' or 'common' working and middle-class people that make up the majority of the population, as opposed to the supposedly **highbrow** educational and cultural elite, who are sometimes said to constitute an embattled and undervalued minority. Popular culture is often said to have a particular appeal to 'the masses' by critics who are opposed to its 'homogenising' and even 'anti-democratic' effects. When writing about the response that the English intelligentsia had to **mass culture** during the early twentieth century, John Carey has argued that the 'metaphor of the mass serves the purposes of individual self-assertion because it turns other people into a conglomerate. It denies them the individuality which we ascribe to ourselves and to people we know' (2002: 21).

Media Tie-In Work of **popular fiction** (usually a novel) commissioned by the rights holder of an existing pop culture property, be it a film, television series, or video game. It could be an expanded novelisation of a screenplay, or a new story based on existing characters and story components. As was the case with the *Star Wars* franchise and *Dr Who*, tie-in novels can help keep interest in a property alive even when the source franchise has stalled. The term also refers to non-fiction publications such as episode guides, encyclopaedias and 'making of' books.

Medical Thriller The medical thriller as we know it today owes much to the considerable success of doctor-turned-author Robin Cook, whose 1977 novel *Coma* combined a 'plucky heroine-in-peril' story with a plot that involved illegal organ harvesting. Cook would go on to write many other thrillers in the same vein. The medical thriller usually features a protagonist with a medical background who works to solve a mystery set wholly or partially within a medical context and/setting. Unauthorised experiments and rogue physicians who play God are common, and the thrills are supplemented by medical terminology. Tess Gerritsen, Peter James and Michael Palmer are more recently associated with the **sub-genre**.

Melodrama Though the term is more often applied to a certain type of Hollywood cinema, which involves big emotions, lavish production values and dramatic story beats, as Nick Daly notes, by the mid-nineteenth century, the melodrama was 'the dominant mode of **popular fiction**. Combining as it did sentiment, suspense, spectacle and morality (2012: 37), John G. Cawelti has also observed that the melodrama does not necessarily belong to any one genre, but rather can incorporate aspects of several different genres. Chief amongst these are the **romance**, family saga, adventure story, combined in a deliberately non-naturalistic fashion, set in 'a world that is purportedly full of the violence and tragedy we associate with "the real world" but that in this case seems to be governed by some benevolent moral principle' (1976: 45).

Meme Term originally coined by Richard Dawkins to describe an idea that passes from one brain to another. Now most widely used to describe any concept, image, character, catchphrase or trope that is spread via the internet, such as the 'Slender Man' mythos.

Men's Adventure Magazines Magazines targeted at a male audience popular in the US between the 1950s and the 1970s. They specialised in lurid 'true stories' with an emphasis on crime, as well as heavily sensationalised accounts of historical episodes, tales of adventure and sex advice. Many of the titles featured eye-catching covers. They were displaced by the increasing presence of pornographic magazines from the early 1970s. The most prominent titles included *Men's Adventure*, *Rage*, *Wildcat Adventures*, *Stag* and *Real Men*.

Midcult Term coined by Dwight Macdonald in 1960. It is essentially another word for '**middlebrow**' – a hybrid form of popular culture that he saw as occupying ground half way between **mass culture** and high culture that 'pretends to respect the standards of High Culture while in fact waters them down and vulgarises them' (2011: 35).

Middlebrow Term which arose in the 1920s and is usually used to describe a form of popular culture which occupies a middle ground between high culture and low or **mass culture**. The middlebrow is often associated with an aspirational middle-class audience. In **popular fiction** studies the term is often used to describe female-authored popular novels written in the UK between the world wars. Nicola Humble emphasises the strong class associations and mutability of the term, and contends that texts move in and out of the category depending on who is reading them, in that having a largely female audience, or considerable commercial popularity can be enough for some commentators to classify a text as 'middlebrow' (2012: 91).

Middle Mind Term coined by Curtis White in 2003. The 'middle mind', argues White, promises intelligence and seriousness but in fact flattens distinctions and 'turns culture into mush', rendering value judgements meaningless. As such, it is said to degrade and impoverish both the imagination and society as a whole. The term resembles Macdonald's earlier conception of '**midcult**'.

Misery Lit Non-fiction genre in which autobiographical tales of great personal hardship and suffering are narrated, often related to terrible abuse and deprivation the author claims to have experienced as a child, although tales of adult addiction, illness and tragedy can also feature.

Mommy Porn Erotic fiction that is supposed to appeal to a female audience in their 30s and 40s. The term was widely used by the media in relation to the massive success of *Fifty Shades of Grey* (2011) and its many imitators.

Mushroom Publishers Term used to describe the many small publishing companies specialising in genre fiction which sprang up in Britain during the post-war period.

N

NaNoWriMo National novel writing month – a popular online challenge which takes place every November, during which participants undertake to write the first draft of a novel (or at least 50,000 words) during the allotted time period.

Net Book Agreement Agreement in 1900 that allowed British publishers to set the retail price of their stock and deny booksellers the right to offer discounted copies. It was declared illegal by the Office for Fair Trade in 1997, when the British publishing industry was deregulated. At this point new sales tactics such as 'loss leaders' (books deliberately under-priced so as to attract customers into shops) and massively discounted copies became possible. These innovations are said by many commentators to have had a particularly negative impact upon smaller and independent booksellers. The end of the NBA also radically changed how author payments were negotiated.

New Adult Fiction Relatively new publishing industry term referring to novels supposedly written for college age readers/recent graduates (aged between 18 and 30) who have begun to 'age out' of **young adult** books. New Adult Fiction tends to deal with protagonists navigating the adult world, relationships, first jobs and so on.

The New Weird Critical term that has emerged since 2000. It is a hybrid **sub-genre** of fantasy that also contains elements of **horror** and **science fiction** and tends to resist conventional generic classification. The roots of the new weird are said to lie in the writing of 'New Wave' science fiction authors such as J. G. Ballard and Jack Vance, as well as Horror writers such as Clive Barker and Thomas Ligotti. Jeff VanderMeer's *Southern Reach* (2014) trilogy has recently been hailed as a masterpiece of the 'new weird'.

Nordic Noir (also known as Scandi Noir) Term used to describe the wave of crime and detective fiction written by Scandinavian authors which rose to global prominence following the immense success of Stieg Larsson's *Millennium* trilogy, the television shows *Forbrydelsen/The Killing* (Denmark, 2007–12) and *Broen/Bron/The Bridge* (a Danish/Swedish co-production, 2011–). A new appetite for Scandinavian crime fiction in English translation paved the way for the publication in English of new authors but also encouraged the translation and reprinting of existing series from writers based in Denmark, Iceland, Sweden and Norway, such as Swedish authors Maj Sjöwell and Per Wahlöö (the team behind the long-running *Martin Beck* series), Henning Mankell (known for the Kurt Wallander series), Norwegian authors Karin Fossum, Jo Nesbø and Anne Holt, and Icelandic author Arnaldur Indriðason who had all amassed an international following before the term began to be widely deployed. The basic characteristics of 'Nordic Noir' include a Scandinavian author and setting and a concern with issues of social justice and state/police corruption

– the dark side of the post-war social democracy is a particular focus of Swedish and Danish crime fiction in particular.

Novelisation Term used when a television series or film script is adapted into a novel format. Novelisations were particularly common when global film release dates were much more staggered than they are now. Most major US film releases would be accompanied by novelisation of the script, sometimes ostensibly written by the original director/writer (as was the case with the novelisation of *Star Wars*, credited to George Lucas but ghost-written by SF author Alan Dean Foster, who has recently also novelised *Star Wars: The Force Awakens*, 2015). Genre television has long benefited from novelisations that explore on-going plot lines or even spin off into new adventures featuring already established characters. A few, more recent TV shows (such as British novelist David Hewson's adaptations of the Danish crime series *The Killing*) have inspired novelisations which can be considered fully realised works of fiction in their own right, as have video games series such as *Halo*. The advent of VHS, DVD and, more recently, digital film downloading has meant that the public appetite for the kind of supplementary material featured in novelisations of the original shooting script has waned considerably.

Nuclear Fiction Hybrid **sub-genre** most notable between the 1950s and the 1980s – the height of the Cold War – which dramatised plot elements and anxieties related to the possession, deployment and use of nuclear weaponry. Nuclear fiction usually combines elements of the techno thriller, apocalyptic fiction and the suspense novel, though not necessarily all in the same novel. Examples include melancholic tales of radiation poisoning such as Nevil Shute's *On the Beach* (1957) and Raymond Briggs's graphic novel *When the Wind Blows* (1982), more hopeful 'rising from the ashes' stories such as Pat Frank's *Alas, Babylon* (1959), and tense tales of diplomatic brinksmanship such as *Fail Safe* (Eugene Burdick and Henry Wheeler, 1962).

P

Paperback Revolution Term used to refer to the process by which paperback books became affordable and widely available. It is particularly associated with Penguin Books Ltd founder Allen Lane, who established the firm in 1935 in order to make sure that ordinary readers would have access to high-quality, intellectually edifying books. The Penguin line from the start combined literary texts and non-fiction titles with works of **popular fiction**, beginning with authors such as Agatha Christie. In the US, publishers such as Fawcett, Pocket Books and Avon were also pivotal in the manufacture and distributing of paperbacks. In 1960, sales of paperback books for the first time exceeded those of hardbacks (Howard 2005: 148).

Paraliterature Term usually associated with French critic Marc Angenot, although it has also been used by other critics, including Leslie Fiedler and Christopher Pawling. It is essentially another way of describing popular/genre fiction, with an emphasis here on the fact that it is a means for **literary fiction** to define itself as what it is *not*. 'Paraliterature' can be described as non-canonical fiction that exists alongside but separate from literary fiction.

Paranormal Romance Hybrid **sub-genre** combining elements of **fantasy, romance** and **horror** in which the (usually female) protagonist finds herself romantically entangled with a male character who is of supernatural or partially supernatural origin. It is also not uncommon for the heroine to have supernatural abilities herself, or to develop them as the series continues. Paranormal romance is one of the major new publishing categories to have emerged since 2000. The paranormal romance boom owes much to the *Twilight* series (2005–8) and its accompanying film adaptations. However, authors whose work predates Stephenie Meyers, such as Laurell K. Hamilton and Charlaine Harris, did much to establish the parameters of the format (even though their fiction is arguably more **urban fantasy** than paranormal romance). Paranormal romance has elements in common with urban fantasy (not least the conceit that there exists a parallel world of supernatural beings existing alongside our own), but whilst romantic entanglements *occasionally* surface in urban fantasy, in paranormal romance, they are *always* the prime narrative focus. In addition, whilst paranormal romance, like romance in general, tends to attract mainly female authors and readers, the urban fantasy has many prominent male authors and many series with male protagonists.

Pen Name Alternative identity adopted by an author who wishes his or her work to be published under a name different from their own. There are various reasons why a writer of **popular fiction** might publish under a pen name. It was once common for female authors to obscure their identities so as to hide the fact that they had taken up the 'unladylike' activity of fiction writing. Hence, the Brontë sisters first published under masculine pen names, whilst Mary Ann Evans became 'George Eliot'. **Science fiction** author 'James Tiptree Jr' was praised for his distinctively 'masculine' writing style before it was revealed that 'he' was actually a woman named Alice B. Sheldon. Sometimes pen names are adopted because an author strongly associated with one genre wishes to write in another. Stephen King published for years as 'Richard Bachman', until his ruse was uncovered by a fan in 1985. More recently, *Harry Potter* author J. K. Rowling attempted a similar feat, but her real identity was leaked shortly after her first crime novel, credited to 'Robert Galbraith', was published. Authors also sometimes use a pen name but publicise their responsibility for the text in question. This is generally a way of signalling that novels written under the alternative persona differ from those usually associated with the author. So, for instance, **romance** novelist Nora Roberts publishes romantic suspense as 'J. D. Robb', Agatha Christie wrote romances under the name 'Mary Westmacott', crime novelist Ruth Rendell wrote psychological thrillers as 'Barbara Vine' and Irish literary novelist John Banville writes 1950s-set crime novels as 'Benjamin Black'.

Penguin Books British firm founded by publishing executive Allen Lane in 1935. Lane wanted to make quality contemporary fiction available to a mass audience at an affordable price. Penguin books were intended to be sold at train stations and chain stores such as Woolworths. Their first list was a combination of **literary fiction** and **popular fiction**. Major imprints soon added: Puffin, which specialised in children's books, began in 1940 whilst the Penguin Classics line, which provided affordable reprints of classic literary texts, was established in 1946. The Penguin Press, which allowed the company to publish in hardback as well as paperback, was established in 1967. Penguin merged with fellow conglomerate Random House in 2012.

Penny Dreadful Cheaply printed, mass-produced serial literature intended primarily for a working-class audience that was particularly popular during the mid- to late- nineteenth century. The material featured in the so-called 'penny dreadfuls' or 'penny bloods' tended towards the lurid, sensationalist, melodramatic and grotesque. These texts were usually published in a pamphlet format and also often featured sensationalist illustrations.

Fictionalised true crime stories were particularly popular, as were reprints of gothic novels. The most famous penny dreadfuls included the Sweeney Todd story *A String of Pearls* (1846–7) and *Varney the Vampire* (1845–7), both written by James Malcolm Rhymer and Thomas Peckett Prest.

Plot One of the main differences between **popular fiction** and **literary fiction** is the importance afforded plot in the former. Plots in popular fiction are often relatively familiar to the reader before they even open the book, at least in outline. When a text belongs to a certain genre or **sub-genre** the reader can reasonably expect the narrative to contain at least some of the typical plot developments associated with that particular genre. For instance, a detective novel demands that there be a crime to be solved, whilst heroic fantasy often involves a quest of some sort and a battle between the forces of good and evil. In popular fiction, plot is generally considered to be more important than language, tone or style. By way of contrast, in literary fiction all of these elements are considered key components of the 'literariness' of a text, and plot is often downplayed. Whereas popular fiction texts are often packed with page-turning incident, it is fairly common for a work of literary fiction to have a relatively sparse plot.

Public Lending Right (PLR) System which allows authors to register and receive payments in return for library loans of their work which operates in most European countries (and is known as the Public Lending Remuneration system in Ireland). It is also a useful means of gauging who are the most commonly borrowed authors in a particular year. At time of writing, thirty-three countries have established a PLR system. The US is not yet amongst them.

Police Procedural **Sub-genre** of crime fiction in which the course and details of the official investigation into a crime (often a murder) forms the main **plot**. The main characters will usually be law enforcement offers working in an official capacity for the state and within the limits of their profession. As Lee Horsley observes, the emphasis 'is on a collaborative process of investigation requiring hierarchical institutional relationships, well-established systems of communication, and shared expertise' (2010: 35).

Popular Modernism Term used by Nicholas Daly to describe the point at which, essentially, **mass culture** and modernism begin to cross over with one another. Daly argues that the work of Victorian **popular fiction** authors such as Stoker, Haggard and Doyle represents an important strand of nascent modernism, and suggests that their fiction was 'formed in the same historical mould as literary modernism' (2000: 9). The term has been applied to the reassessment of modernism in order to consider the movement's engagement with mass publication outlets (many of the leading authors also frequently published in mass-market popular magazines) as well as the relationship between modernism and popular genres, with particular attention being paid to so-called 'pulp modernism' supposedly epitomised by the writing of authors such as Raymond Chandler.

Popular Fiction see Introduction for a detailed definition

Posthumous Publication Posthumous publication occurs when a work of fiction is published for the first time after the death of the author. Within a **popular fiction** context there have been some notable examples of posthumous publication. Stieg Larsson died shortly before the *Millennium* trilogy (originally published between 2005 and 2007) made him one of the best-selling authors in the world. James Bond creator Ian Fleming's final novel, *The Man with the Golden Gun* (1965) and short fiction collection *Octopussy and the Living Daylights* (1966) were also published after his death. More recently, the final 'Discworld' novel, *The Shepherd's Crown* (2015) was published after the death of author Terry Pratchett. Sometimes a work partially finished before the author's death is completed by another writer or editor, as was the case with J. R. R. Tolkien's *The Silmarillion* (1977), which was prepared for publication by his son, Christopher.

Potboiler A work of fiction supposedly written for purely financial motives, containing sensational plot elements contrived to appeal to the widest possible audience.

Print-On-Demand (POD) Companies offering print-on-demand services print books in hard copy format once firm orders have been received (rather than printing in advance of orders, as is the usual practice within publishing). Such services have become more popular in recent years thanks to the rise in the number of authors who are **self-publishing** and self-promoting, because POD allows for small and relatively inexpensive initial print runs. Major POD platforms at time of writing include Lulu Press, Smashwords and the **Amazon**-owned CreateSpace, which also hosts a digital publishing platform, and therefore allows authors to sell their work as **e-books** and in hard copy.

Pro-Fic Professional Fiction. Term used within **fanfiction** circles to refer to professionally published and commercially sold works.

Pulp Fiction Cheap, disposable and readily available genre fiction, published in **magazine, dime novel** or **paperback** novel format, usually with colourful cover art. Pulp fiction is named after the cheap wood pulp that was used to make the paper these kinds of texts were initially printed on. However, as Lee Server notes, the term 'pulp' soon came to encompass both a categorical and aesthetic meaning as well:

> pulp as a genus of imaginative reading matter distinguished by mass production, affordability, an intended audience of common as opposed to elite readers, a dependence on formula and genre; and pulp as literature aimed at the pleasure centres of the reader, primarily concerned with sensation and escape, variously intended to excite, astonish or arouse. (2009: xi)

The heyday of pulp fiction occurred between the late-nineteenth century and the mid-twentieth century. Certain genres achieved particular success during the pulp era, amongst them the **western, crime** (in particular **hard-boiled detective fiction**), true crime, **science fiction, weird fiction** and adventure stories. The term 'pulp fiction' is also sometimes used to describe **popular fiction** more generally (as in Scott McCracken's *Pulp: Reading Popular Fiction*, 1998).

R

Remediation Process by which one form of technological medium begins to replace or improve upon another that performs a similar role. Jay David Bolter argues for instance that 'Digital technology is turning out to be one of the more traumatic remediations in the history of western writing' (2001: 24).

Revenant Bestseller Term used by John Sutherland to describe a book which returns to the **bestseller** lists after being out of them for more than a year.

Romance see entry in Major Popular Genres section

Romantic Suspense **Sub-genre** of the **romance** novel including a strong element of mystery/jeopardy alongside the main love story plot. Romantic suspense is often said to have been pioneered by the British author Mary Stewart, and is now most famously associated with Nora Roberts, who publishes her romantic suspense novels as 'J. D. Robb'.

| S |

School Story Sub-genre of children's literature/**YA** fiction which has a school setting – often a British public school in which children are boarders. The typical school story follows a naïve young pupil encountering the rules and rituals of the place for the first time, with the plot often being shaped by the structure of a school term. One of the most significant early school stories is the Victorian bestseller *Tom Brown's School Days* (1857) by Thomas Hughes, which followed the protagonist from initial entry as a terrified youngster to his triumphant departure as a well-rounded young gentleman. Authors such as Enid Blyton, Elinor Brent Dwyer, Diana Wynne-Jones and J. K. Rowling have written school stories, in the latter two instances combining them with fantastical elements. There is also a long tradition of American high-school set tales in both popular film and fiction (and even a few boarding school narratives), but these tend to differ substantially from their British counterparts.

Science Fiction see entry in Major Popular Genres section

Scientific Romance Term used in the UK to describe the imaginative tales of adventure, innovation and scientific invention written by authors such as H. G. Wells. As Brian Stableford notes, the term never caught on in the US because Hugo Gernsback's alternative descriptor '**science fiction**' was soon widely deployed there instead (2006: 468).

Scientific Thriller Sub-genre of the **thriller** in which the main premise is related to a threat posed by a new scientific innovation or discovery. Mary Shelley's *Frankenstein* (1818) is arguably one of the first novels of this type. Michael Crichton, author of *The Andromeda Strain* (1969), *Jurassic Park* (1990) and *Prey* (2002) helped establish the template for the modern day scientific thriller.

Self-Publishing Process by which an author decides to bypass traditional publication models and oversee the publishing, distribution and marketing of their own work. The self-publishing market has been boosted by the electronic publishing boom, which facilitated the establishment of e-publishing platforms such as **Amazon Kindle Direct**, **Wattpad** and Smashwords. It is now not uncommon for authors whose work was initially self-published online (such as **science fiction** authors Hugh Howey and Andy Weir and **paranormal romance** author Amanda Hocking) to be picked up by mainstream publishers after their work has attracted a substantial following.

Sensation Fiction A variety of **popular fiction** that emerged in Victorian Britain during the mid-nineteenth century and afterwards. As Pamela K. Gilbert observes, 'the new genre was distinctively transgressive in that it was thought to appeal directly to the 'nerves', eliciting a physical sensation with its surprises, plot twists and startling revelations' (2011: 2). Sensation fiction helped pave the way for the present day **thriller**. It was immensely popular in Britain from the 1860s onwards, and was associated with writers such as Mary Elizabeth Braddon, Ellen Wood, Charles Dickens (whose fiction often contained distinctively 'sensational' elements) and Wilkie Collins, author of *The Moonstone* (1868) and *The Woman in White* (1860). Sensation novels frequently dramatised themes that were considered too lurid to be openly spoken of, such as madness, murder, spousal abuse and illegitimacy.

Serial Killer Thriller Since the publication of Thomas Harris's *The Silence of the Lambs* (1988), the serial killer thriller has established itself as one of the most popular varieties of the **thriller** (although many of these novels could, like the work of Harris, arguably also be categorised as **horror** novels: the generic lines are often blurred). Many present-day serial killer thrillers imitate the basic plot structure first used by Harris, interweaving chapters told from the killer's perspective (which reveal the aberrant psychological compulsions and tormented backstory that have made him or her into a killer, as well as the planning and execution of their latest gruesome murder) with chapters focusing on the law enforcement officers determined to bring the antagonist to justice. There are also thrillers/horror novels told entirely or mainly from the perspective of the killer, such as Jim Thompson's 1952 noir classic *The Killer Inside Me*, Robert Bloch's *Psycho* (1959), John Fowles's 1963 debut novel *The Collector*, (a major influence on Harris), Bret Easton Ellis's *American Psycho* (1991) and Jeff Lindsay's *Dexter* series (2004–15). Mark Seltzer has persuasively suggested that 'serial murder and its representations have by now largely replaced the Western as the most popular genre-fiction of the body and of bodily violence in our culture' (1998: 1).

Serialisation Until the beginning of the twentieth century, many **popular fiction** narratives were published in serial form, usually weekly or monthly, one chapter (or volume) at a time. It was in an author's best commercial interest to string the audience along for as long as possible: serialised stories therefore often ended with a dramatic twist or cliff-hanger intended to keep the reader hooked until the next instalment. As Christopher Lindner notes, 'we owe the phenomenon of the serial to Victorian England, where the rise of mass production, cheap printing, public literacy, professional authorship and modern advertising created the conditions needed for launching mass media and the modern periodical' (2014: X). Some contemporary authors of popular fiction have also experimented with serialisation. Stephen King initially published his 1996 novel *The Green Mile* in six parts and would become an electronic publishing pioneer with his serialised **e-book** *The Plant* (2000). More recently, David Mitchell's haunted house tale *Slade House* (2015) began life as a series of tweets. The immediacy and accessibility of **e-publishing** lends itself particularly well to serialisation, and **fanfiction** is also often published in a serial format. **Amazon** has recently set up the **Kindle Serials** program, and **Wattpad** is organised around the idea that authors should publish their work in short, regular bursts. Novels have also been distributed as serialised text messages, particularly in China and Japan.

'Serious' Literature Alternative descriptor for **literary fiction**, which implies that whilst this kind of writing carries intellectual weight and artistic ambition, **popular fiction** is lightweight and fundamentally 'unserious'.

'Sad Puppies' Controversy Dispute related to nominations for the ballots of the 2015 Hugo Awards for excellence in **science fiction**. The controversy began with an organised voting campaign masterminded by politically conservative fans/writers/publishers who believed that recent voting patterns had reflected a bias on the part of the organisers towards fiction of a more socially 'progressive' and 'message driven' nature. (The name 'Sad Puppies' was intended as joking reference to a supposedly mawkish charity advertisement.) It was also argued that some prominent recent winners had reflected **highbrow** 'literary' aspirations and left-wing political leanings rather than true 'popular taste'. The 'Sad Puppies', and their even more vociferous 'Rabid Puppies' allies flooded the ballot with nominees whose work represented their own ideas of what science fiction should be like. Ultimately, Hugo voters overwhelmingly rejected the 'Sad Puppies' slate of nominees, preferring to vote instead for the 'No Award' option in many categories.

Shared World/Universe Fictional universe shaped by the input of more than one creator/contributor. The term is used in the comic-book industry to refer to the shared worlds/universes populated by the heroes and villains who make up the Marvel and DC universes respectively (Marvel even has a 'Marvel Cinematic Universe' that ties together its big screen properties). Shared worlds are particularly common in **science fiction** and **fantasy** (see for instance the ever-expanding *Star Wars* and *Star Trek* franchises, or Joss Whedon's 'Buffyverse').

Shelf-Life The amount of time that a work of **popular fiction** remains commercially available and/or culturally prominent.

'Sick Lit' **Sub-genre** of **YA** that focuses upon a protagonist who has a serious or life-threatening medical or psychological condition.

Slash Fanfiction term referring to a 'fic' (or story) that posits a romantic and/or sexual relationship between characters who were not involved in the source text. Slash often pairs two (or more) characters of the same sex.

Small-press Publishing Small presses have always been of particular importance for certain genres and **sub-genres**. The present-day prominence of **weird fiction** author H. P. Lovecraft owes much to the dedication of Arkham House, for instance, whilst one of the leading publishers of short-form **horror** fiction in the US is Cemetery Dance Publications. Tartarus Press, Valancourt Books and Swan River Press all specialise in reprinting both new and classic/neglected supernatural, horror and fantastic fiction. Bizarro Fiction was first established by the likes of Raw Dog Screaming Press and Eraserhead Press. Small press publishing facilitates the distribution, publication and republication of genre fiction that would otherwise be underserved (or ignored) by the mainstream publishing industry.

Space Opera When people unfamiliar with **SF** think of the genre, it is probably the tropes and visuals of the Space Opera that come to mind. As noted in *The Encyclopaedia of Science Fiction*, although the term initially applied to hackneyed and stereotypical **pulp fiction**s, as the 1940s progressed, it began to 'be applied instead to colourful action adventure stories of interplanetary or interstellar conflict' (Clute and Nicholls 1999: 1138). Many of the most significant SF narratives of the late twentieth century and early twenty-first century can be described as 'Space Operas'. These include *Star Wars* (1977), the *Star Trek* (1966–) franchise, and much of the work of Robert Heinlein, Isaac Asimov and Arthur C. Clarke (and a multitude of other major writers from the Golden age and after, such as Lois McMaster Bujold, Iain M. Banks and Peter S. Hamilton). Notable recent examples include the acclaimed TV series *Battlestar Galactica* (2004–9) and the film *Interstellar* (2014). Ann Leckie's 2013 novel *Ancillary Justice* was widely hailed as a particularly ambitious addition to the space opera canon. The **sub-genre**'s fondness for vaguely martial tales of derring-do, visits to exotic planets, space battles and spaceships means that it has always lent itself particularly well to the visual medium.

Speculative Fiction Loosely defined term generally used as an alternative (albeit controversial) descriptor for **science fiction** and **fantasy** (and sometimes non-realist fiction in general). Some writers and fans associated with the SF genre in particular have suggested that the term is deployed by writers from a more self-consciously 'literary' tradition who wish to publicly distance themselves from the genre whose conventions they are themselves appropriating. Although well-known SF authors such as Robert Heinlein and Samuel Delaney have also used the term in reference to their own work, it is nowadays perhaps most associated with Margaret Atwood, who has said that because her works in this vein dramatise events that *might* happen in the future, they are speculative rather than science fictional (she associates the genre with more fantastical and overtly outlandish elements).

Steampunk Sub-genre of **science fiction** usually set in an alternative version of Victorian Britain in which technological developments are much more advanced than they were in historical actuality. Important early works include *The Difference Engine* by William Gibson and Bruce Sterling (1990) and *Infernal Devices* by K. W. Jeter (1987), which, like *The Mechanical* by Ian Tregillis (2015), features clockwork automata.

Steampunk has undergone a major pop culture renaissance in recent years, in part thanks to the rich possibilities it presents for various forms of cosplay. Female authors have produced many of the most notable recent mass-market steampunk novels, with Gail Carriger, Lilith Saintcrow and Meljean Brook all having authored multi-volume series which combine Steampunk with **romance** and **fantasy** elements. Although many, if not most, Steampunk tales are set in a fictionalised version of Victorian London, there are some examples set in an alternative version of our own time, such as *The Fall of the Gas Lit Empire* series by Rod Duncan (2014–) (which features a version of Britain that split up into two very different realms as a result of a successful Luddite rebellion), and titles set in a steampunk version of nineteenth-century North America, such as Cherie Priest's *Clockwork Century* series (2009–).

Street Lit Term used in the US to describe gritty, authentic and uncompromising stories of life on the streets. The term has mainly been associated with African-American authors who feel that the lives of those living in poorer, disenfranchised neighbourhoods have been ignored by 'mainstream' (i.e. white) literary culture. 'Street Lit' authors often use pen-names. The terms 'Urban Literature' and 'Hip-Hop Fiction' are sometimes also used in reference to these novels.

Sub-Genre A sub-genre is a recognisable sub-category existing within a particular genre. Every major popular genre has multiple sub-genres. The existence of sub-genre is also a way for readers, publishers and bookshops to further refine and respond to reader interests. Publishers specialising in one particular genre – e.g. **romance** – usually have imprints catering to specific sub-genres within that umbrella category, such as 'erotica', or 'paranormal romance'.

Superhero Fiction Whilst the superhero has been a mainstay of the comic book since the late 1930s, it is only relatively recently that they have made substantial inroads into prose fiction. The current popularity of the superhero novel was preceded by Bantam's long-running *Wild Cards* anthology series (which began in 1987, and was co-edited for many years by George R. R. Martin), set in an alternative history version of post-World War II Earth in which an alien virus creates a multitude of superheroes and super-villains. Although some superhero novels, such as crime author Andrew Vachss's *Batman: The Ultimate Evil* (1995) and Tom De Haven's *It's Superman!* (2011), are authorised takes on established characters, in recent years quite a few original superhero origin stories

have been released as novels, many of them affectionately decon-
structing the very conceit of the superhero. These include: Austin
Grossman's *Soon I Will Be Invincible* (2007); Kelly Thompson's
depiction of female superhero who is inextricably linked to her
gleefully insane nemesis in *The Girl Who Would be King* (2013);
Lavie Tidhar's decade-spanning *The Violent Century* (2013),
V. E. Schwab's *Vicious* (2013) and Brandon Sanderson's YA
Steelheart series (2013–16). These novels, like their comic-book
counterparts, tend to focus on themes of power, morality and
social responsibility.

Supermarket Fiction Like the terms **airport novel** and **drugstore
paperback,** the term 'Supermarket Fiction' refers to mass-market paperbacks sold outside of bookstores, in this instance, in
supermarkets/superstores.

Super Thursday Important date for the British publishing industry.
'Super Thursday' (usually in mid-October) is when the initial
details of the new titles that will be released in time for the
Christmas buying boom are released.

Suspense 'Suspense' is a rather nebulous publishing category that
often crosses over into **crime,** mystery and even **romance,** but can
also have elements in common with **horror** and **gothic** fiction. As
the name would suggest, suspense novels are primarily supposed
to evoke tension and anticipation in the reader. These kinds of
novels often feature plots in which the protagonist is drawn into
a mystery and faces considerable personal jeopardy. Vicarious
identification with the embattled protagonist's situation is a key
aspect of such narratives. Like the **thriller** (a close relative) the
suspense novel is a descendant of **sensation fiction.** Noël Carroll
usefully notes that it is generally agreed that 'a key component
of the emotion *suspense* is a state of cognitive uncertainty.
We feel suspense as the heroine heads for the buzzsaw, in part
because we are uncertain as to whether or not she will be cleaved'
(2013: 71).

Sword and Sorcery Fantasy sub-genre (particularly associated with
the American pulp magazines of the 1930s and 1940s), which
generally involved sword-wielding protagonists and the use of
magic. The conventions of the Sword and Sorcery tale were established by authors such as Robert E. Howard, Fritz Leiber and
C. L. Moore. The sub-genre has arguably since been absorbed
into 'epic' or 'heroic' fantasy. Sword and Sorcery was however

a major influence upon the RPG (role playing game) trend of the 1970s and after.

| T |

Technothriller Thriller characterised by a plot containing rogue or dangerous technological innovations, often a featuring a device that has some kind of potentially devastating military application. Tom Clancy's 1984 bestseller *The Hunt for Red October* helped establish the **sub-genre** in its current incarnation. His intensely detailed descriptions of military hardware and equipment particularly appealed to readers looking for 'insider information'.

Textual Poaching Term that originates with Michel de Certeau. In *The Practice of Everyday Life* (1984) he argues that rather than just being passive consumers of **mass culture**, people are in fact actively engaging the text in question, and even appropriate this material for their own use and interpretation (2011: 174). In other words, they are 'poachers'. This position on mass culture contrasts with that of thinkers such as Adorno, for whom the popular audience is a much more passive and malleable entity. The term is also associated with the **fandom** scholar Henry Jenkins, who expands upon de Certeau's ideas in his book *Textual Poachers: Television Fans and Participatory Culture* (1993).

Thrillers see entry in Major Popular Genres section

Trade Paperback Softcover book commercially pitched somewhere between a **hardback** and a **mass-market paperback**. Trade paperbacks are more expensive, slightly larger and generally of better quality (and hence more collectable) than the latter, but more affordable than the former.

Trope Within a **popular fiction** context, a trope is a standard, familiar (and occasionally clichéd) story element, setting, theme or plot device that authors operating within a particular genre characteristically return to again and again. These include the likes of the haunted house (a staple of **horror/supernatural** fiction); the plucky heroine who battles a totalitarian regime (a staple of recent **YA dystopian fiction**), the gunslinger (**westerns**), or the hard-bitten detective (mystery/noir/**crime**).

True Crime Non-fiction genre concerned with factual accounts of real-life criminal acts, both solved and unsolved. True crime as we understand the term today has its roots in eighteenth-century publications such as the 'Newgate Calendar', which collected together accounts of the life stories and criminal deeds of prisoners awaiting execution in London's Newgate Prison. Broadsheets, chapbooks and **penny dreadfuls** often drew on true crimes, as did ballads and oral recitations. **Popular fiction** has long been inspired by true crimes. The first major American **gothic** novel, Charles Brockden Brown's *Wieland: An American Tale* (1798), was based upon a real-life family massacre that took place in upstate New York in 1781. Wilkie Collins's classic **sensation novel** *The Moonstone* (1868) appropriated elements of the infamous 1860 'Road Hill House' child murder, as did the 1862 bestseller *Lady Audley's Secret* by Mary Elizabeth Braddon, whilst Shirley Jackson's *We Have Always Lived in the Castle* (1962) fictionalises aspects of the 1892 Lizzy Borden case. The crimes of Wisconsin murderer and grave-robber Ed Gein not only inspired Robert Bloch's ground-breaking psychological thriller *Psycho* (1959), but also influenced *The Silence of the Lambs* (1988). Truman Capote claimed to have created an entirely new genre – the 'non fiction novel' in his classic account of the slaying of a Kansas farm family, *In Cold Blood* (1966). A similar approach to a high-profile crime was used by Norman Mailer in *The Executioner's Song* (1979); it was anticipated by Meyer Levin's fictionalisation of the 'Leopold and Loeb' case in *Compulsion* (1956). Anne Rule's account of her relationship with Ted Bundy in *The Stranger Beside Me* (1980) helped establish a thriving market for mass-market true crime books focusing on the exploits of serial killers. For obvious reasons, **crime** novels also often draw upon real-life incidents. Neo-noir writer James Ellroy specialises in incorporating actual historical events and figures into his LA-set crime novels, most famously in *The Black Dahlia* (1987). More recently, Gillian Flynn has stated that her **domestic noir** mega-hit *Gone Girl* (2012) was influenced by the media coverage of high-profile spousal murder cases. Within popular culture more broadly, the popularity and media attention given to the first season of the immersive podcast *Serial* (2015–) and the TV series *The Jinx* (2015) and *The Making of a Murderer* (2015) underline the fact that true crime is currently experiencing a major surge of popularity across the media landscape.

Twi-Mom Term applied to the women well above **YA** age category who are avid fans of the *Twilight* series in both book and film form.

Twitterature Short fiction published on Twitter social media platform in bursts of 140 characters or less.

U

Urban Fantasy Sub-genre of **fantasy** which also contains elements of **horror**, action, mystery and, occasionally, noir. As Peter S. Beagle writes, 'Urban fantasy counts on familiarity with mythology, fairytales, and the earliest horror tropes, like vampires, werewolves and warlocks [...] as shorthand to pull the reader through familiar territory quickly without wasting precious time' (2011: 11). The setting is always a major city (usually one that also exists in real life) in which all manner of fantastical and supernatural entities and events exist alongside a more recognisably mundane 'real world'. The protagonist is usually a hard-bitten, cynical, ass-kicking detective figure who is either drawn into this underworld or already belongs to it. Exotic love interests are a regular feature, but unlike as in **paranormal romance**, this is not the prime focus of narrative interest. Television shows such as *Buffy the Vampire Slayer* (1997–2003), *Angel* (1999–2004) and *Supernatural* (2005–) have been major influences on the contemporary urban fantasy.

Utopian Fiction A utopian story is set in an imagined world that purports to be the 'ideal' society, or at least is attempting to be so. The word 'utopia' (coined in 1516 by Sir Thomas More) is derived from the Greek for both 'no place' and 'good place' and stands as one of the earliest and most common forms of proto-**science fiction**. Like its grim twin, the Dystopian story, the utopian tale is usually a platform for the author to express their own political and philosophical beliefs and predictions, in order to dramatise their own vision of societal perfection. Although **dystopian fictions** are much more common in contemporary popular culture, both the *Star Trek* universe and Iain M. Banks *Culture* novels represent striking visions of a utopian future. Dave Egger's 2013 novel *The Circle* is a satirical and timely take on the common 'this supposedly utopian society is actually quite dystopian' narrative trope.

V

Video Games As electronic gaming has become accepted as an ever more technologically sophisticated facet of popular culture, video game narratives have become richer and more immersive. The idea of **genre** within video games is very different from the concept as it exists in fiction, in that here, generic categories describe particular types of gameplay and game structure (such as 'MMORPG' [massively multiplayer online role-playing game], 'First Person Shooter' and 'Platformer'). Nevertheless, games makers have created many titles that belong to recognisable **popular fiction** genres, in particular **horror, science fiction**, adventure and mystery. Gaming culture has also inspired a number of works of popular fiction, including Ernest Cline's *Ready Player One* (2011) and *Armada* (2015), as well as novels based on popular games series such as *Halo*, *Metal Gear Solid* and *Assassin's Creed*.

| W |

Wattpad Online publishing platform, established in 2006, that describes itself as 'the world's largest community of readers and writers'. It hosts free-to-access stories related to every conceivable **genre, sub-genre** and variety of **fanfiction**. Writers – by and large amateurs – create an online profile linked to the site, and then amass followers by engaging with fans in the comments sections, promoting their work online through social media, and regularly adding new work. Writers are encouraged to provide their followers with new chapters on a regular, serialised basis. Chapters are often quite short, presented as unpolished or even initial drafts, and end on cliff-hangers in order to whet the reader's appetite for further instalments. Some Wattpad authors, such as *One Direction* fanfiction author Anna Todd, have amassed followings so sizable that they have subsequently been signed up by major (offline) publishers. Wattpad is a particularly popular online publication medium for teenagers and young women.

Web Fiction Fiction written for initial or sole publication online, either for self-publishing platforms such as **Wattpad** and **Kindle Direct,** personal blogs, Livejournal, or sites such as CreepyPasta. com and **fanfiction** forums.

Web Serial Work of serialised fiction initially made available online only.

Weird Fiction/The Weird Tale A hybrid generic term that is primarily associated with the work of a specific set of authors that emerged from the American pulp magazines of the 1930s and 1940s, in particular, *Weird Tales*. Weird fiction can be loosely defined as fiction that combines elements from **horror, fantasy** and **science fiction**, although, as S. T. Joshi argues, 'no definition of the weird tale embraces all types of works that can plausibly be assumed to enter into the scope of the term' (1990: 2). What is agreed upon is that one of weird fiction's major authors is H. P. Lovecraft (whose 1927 essay 'Supernatural Horror in Literature' is a key theoretical rumination on 'the weird tradition'). In their 2011 anthology *The Weird: A Compendium of Strange and Dark Stories*, Jeff and Anne VanderMeer argue that in order to qualify as truly 'weird' a tale must fundamentally be about our relationship with what we know as reality.

The Western The Western emerged from the **dime novels** and **pulp magazines** of mid–late nineteenth-century America. From roughly the beginning of the twentieth century until the late 1960s, the Western was one of the major popular genres, dominating **popular fiction**, television and cinema. As Stephen Matterson observes,

> The Western is, broadly, any literary work set on the frontier that involves conflicts between groups over the future ownership or usage of the land [. . .] Westerns also frequently explore the nature of individual heroism and of manliness, with the frontier being recognised as a space where manhood can be fully expressed beyond the domesticating influence of women. (2003: 236)

Authors associated with the 'Golden Age' of the Western include Owen Wister (author of *The Virginian* [1902], which is cited by John Cawelti as the beginning of the modern western), Louis L'Amour and Zane Grey. More recently, Larry McMurtry and Cormac McCarthy have written elegiac and revisionist narratives in this vein.

'Women in Refrigerators' Phrase coined by **comic** book writer Gail Simone in response to an infamous 1994 issue of *Green Lantern* in which the male protagonist's girlfriend was murdered and shoved into the aforementioned domestic appliance. Simone and a number of other figures working in the comics industry set up an influential website of the same name dedicated to highlighting the frequency with which the abuse, threats and murder of female characters were used against male protagonists. Their wider mission was to encourage the creation of female characters who are well rounded characters in their own right and exist for reasons other than to be used as a weapon against the male hero (or 'fridged').

Women's Fiction Controversial term used to refer to certain types of **popular fiction** written by female authors and read by a predominantly female audience. Some authors have rejected the label because they see it as a way of downplaying the importance of female-authored texts and dismissing their treatment of subjects such as domestic life, intimate relationships and marriage. It has been argued that the term feeds into the condescending perception that whilst male authors write 'big', ambitious novels about 'weighty' topics, women write on a small scale about 'women's issues'. The 'Women's Fiction' chapter of the RWA (Romance Writers of America) however defines it as 'as a commercial novel about a woman on the brink of life change and personal growth. Her journey details emotional reflection and action that transforms her and her relationships with others, and includes a hopeful/upbeat ending with regard to her romantic relationship', although their placement under the umbrella of 'romance' fiction arguably means that these novels are more likely to have a conventionally 'happy' conclusion. In contrast, whilst Jodi Picoult also identifies herself as a writer of 'Women's Fiction', her books typically deal with morally complex and even taboo subjects, such as the ethics of conceiving a child so that they can act as a 'saviour sibling' (*My Sister's Keeper*, 2004); the aftermath of a high-school shooting (*Nineteen Minutes*, 2007) and the Holocaust (*The Storyteller*, 2013).

World-Building Process by which an author creates a fully realised and immersive fictional universe. World-building is considered particularly important in **genre**s which often are set in secondary worlds, such as **fantasy** and **science fiction**, although it arguably occurs in any work of fiction.

| Y |

Young Adult Fiction (YA) Broadly defined commercial publishing category that emerged in the US in the late 1960s. The term 'Young Adult' is generally used to describe fiction targeted at readers aged between roughly 12 and 20, although since 2000 it has become clear that many of the most vociferous readers of YA are much older. The 1967 publication of S. E. Hinton's troubled-teen novel *The Outsiders* is generally cited as one of the starting points for YA as a distinct publishing category (Hill 2013: 1). A work of YA fiction can conceivably belong to any popular **Genre**. There are also **sub-genre**s specifically associated with YA, such as 'sick lit' (epitomised by John Green's bestseller *The Fault in Our Stars* (2012), although novels featuring seriously ill teen protagonists were popular even in the 1980s) and, more recently, 'Real-Life' YA, which represents a move away from the **fantasy** and **dystopian** trend and towards conflicts and issues of a more everyday, 'real world' kind. YA fiction is now one of the most commercially dominant varieties of **popular fiction**, and film and TV adaptations of such texts have also become increasingly significant.

Z

Zombie Lit Sub-genre of **horror/apocalyptic fiction** set in a world in which a zombie outbreak has devastated humanity. Literary depictions of the modern, post *Night of the Living Dead* (1968) zombie were, with the exceptions of stories featured in a few notable anthologies (such as John Skipp and Craig Spector's *Book of the Dead* [1989]), quite rare until post-2000. However, the 'mainstreaming' of the zombie which followed the success of the *Resident Evil* (1996–) videogame series, the 'oral history' *World War Z* (2006) and the **comic** book/TV series *The Walking Dead* (2003–) means that the living dead have now shuffled into the realms of **popular fiction** as well, thanks to authors such as David Moody, David Wellington, Mira Grant, M. R. Carey and Alden Bell. In a further example of the so-called **genrefication** of US **literary fiction**, Colson Whitehead's *Zone One* (2011) was favourably received by both critics and readers. The main themes of zombie lit include the quest to rebuild a functioning society, the psychological and moral cost of surviving in a world without order or safety, and questions about whether or not humanity even deserves to continue. The greatest threat usually comes from the stupidity, insanity and avarice of other survivors, rather than from the undead. All zombie lit owes a massive debt to the work of writer/director George A. Romero, whose 'Living Dead' films created our conception of the modern zombie narrative.

Key Critical and Theoretical Approaches to Popular Fiction

The following section is intended to provide a concise introduction to nine key and emerging critical and theoretical approaches to popular fiction. It also provides a broad overview of the historical development of academic approaches to the subject. The entries that follow are *not* intended to serve as exhaustive or definitive discussions of the academic perspectives under discussion. Rather, they represent an accessible starting point for more advanced critical reading and study, and will also only discuss specific critical approaches in relation to how they have been applied to representative examples of popular fiction, not literature in general.

1. Liberal Humanism and the Cambridge English School

Proponents of literary studies during the late nineteenth and early twentieth centuries were very conscious of claims that the subject did not represent a fitting topic for rigorous academic study. As a result, there was a need to justify the enduring importance of literature and to support the case that it was as valid a subject of serious intellectual inquiry as mathematics, philosophy or the sciences. The first major movement within literary studies was therefore what John Storey calls the 'culture and civilisation tradition', which tended to take a very moralistic and human-centred view of literature (2009: 18). The idea was that the study of what was classified as 'good' literature not only made one a better person on an individual level, it also helped create a defence against the dehumanising and even chaotic forces of modernity. Accompanying this sense of moral and intellectual mission was a correspondingly narrow view of what literature is, and how it should best be studied. Needless to say, works that we would now classify as 'popular fiction' were, in a sign of things to come for many decades after, not usually considered either as 'good' or as proper 'literature'.

What would become known as the liberal humanist approach was greatly influenced by the work of poet and critic Matthew Arnold, who in *Culture and Anarchy* (1867–9) famously characterised culture as 'the best which has been thought and said in the world' (2006: 5). Writing at a time of considerable social, economic and political change for the United Kingdom, Arnold saw culture as a balm for an increasingly chaotic and even morally diseased age dominated by 'machinery'. He also believed that culture was of particular importance in terms of how it could positively influence the ever-expanding ranks of the middle classes (2006: 55).

Arnold's writings had an important influence upon the so-called 'Cambridge English School' of the 1920s. Of particular interest to the student of popular fiction is the work of husband and wife team F. R. (Frank) and Q. D. (Queenie, *née* Roth) Leavis. For the Leavises, there was no doubt that the study of literature made one a better human being. 'High' culture in general and 'good' literature in particular were seen as the last lines of defence for a civilisation in possibly terminal decline. Particularly important is F. R. Leavis's 1930 pamphlet 'Mass Civilisation and Minority Culture', in which he argues that only an educated minority can discerningly appreciate art and literature, and are capable of 'unprompted, first-hand judgement' (2011: 143). This minority is extremely important, he continues, because upon them depends 'our power of profiting by the finest human experience of the past' (2011: 144). This intellectual elite not only create the evaluative standards by which culture can be appraised but also uphold the moral and philosophical ideals that 'order the finer living of the age' (2011: 144).

F. R. Leavis's belief that culture was in a state of unprecedented crisis is one that we see echoed again and again in much subsequent critical writing on the relationship between 'mass' and 'high' culture. So too was his contention that culture was at that time under major threat from mass production, standardisation and a process of 'levelling down' (2011: 147). Indeed, as we shall see, precisely this kind of terminology arises over and over again in the work of critics and commentators for whom the 'harmful' effects of 'mass' culture is a given. Like Theodor Adorno and Max Horkheimer a few years later, F. R. Leavis singled out the then relatively new medium of film for sustained critique (Pease 2011: 203). Both film and radio, he argued, negatively impact upon the ability of the individual to know and to effectively use their own minds due to their reliance upon the creation of cheap emotional response rather than genuine emotional or intellectual engagement. As Alison Pease notes, in F. R. Leavis's characterisation, 'the typical consumer of mass culture in the 1920s and 1930s was understood to be an emotionally stunted, passive receptacle with an endless capacity to be filled with cheap, repetitive media' (2011: 203). Indeed, the mass audience, in his reading, is so overwhelmed by the sheer range of bewildering signals that, as Leavis puts it, 'unless he is especially gifted or especially favoured, he can hardly begin to discriminate. Here we have the plight of culture in general. The landmarks have shifted, multiplied and crowded upon one another, the distinctions and dividing lines have blurred away, the boundaries are gone'. Faced with what he suggestively calls 'a smother of new books', only a very small proportion of the general public – the masses – is realistically able to cope (2011: 159). Interestingly, Leavis uses an example specifically related to the growth of popular fiction – the American Book-of-the-Month club – as an example of the fact that the reader these days now needs to be spoon-fed from a selection of pre-selected tomes.

F. R. Leavis remains one of the most significant literary critics of the twentieth century, and is also well known for his idiosyncratic take on the development of the English novel in *The Great Tradition* (1948). Just as important is the work of his wife Q. D. Leavis, whose pioneering study *Fiction and the Reading Public* (1932) represents one of the earliest academic attempts to scrutinise popular fiction. It is also, as David Ayers notes, 'a polemical work which aims to rally the cultured "minority", a group which she regrets is now to be distinguished from the powerful minority since "the people with power no longer represent intellectual authority and culture"' (Ayers 2004: 117).

Q. D. Leavis upheld fundamental Leavisite values such as the belief that there existed a (sadly past) 'Golden Age' during which the balance between an enlightened mass readership and uplifting and significant forms of literature was just about right. Utilising what she called an 'anthropological' method of investigation (which included sending questionnaires to sixty of the most successful contemporary best-selling authors, twenty-five of whom responded), Q. D. Leavis's deployment of historical context and discussion of the commercial conditions that help shape popular reading habits in both the past and present was extremely influential, even if, as John Docker notes, she makes it clear from the outset that she does not believe that popular fiction warrants the kind of close reading that 'proper' literature deserves (1994: 24).

Q. D. Leavis argued that innovations such as cheap circulating libraries and magazines specialising in popular fiction had accustomed the British public to a certain kind of undemanding, escapist reading material which left them completely unprepared (and unwilling) to engage with the tragically neglected 'good' literature of the age. In what would become an often-replicated characterisation, the affordable thrillers that were particularly popular at the time were described as a 'form of drug habit' (1979: 22) that appealed to the average reader because they 'excite an emotional activity for which there is no scope in his life' (1979: 63). She further suggested that fiction by authors such as the famous late Victorian popular writers Marie Corelli and Hall Caine 'actually get in the way of genuine feeling and responsible thinking by creating cheap mechanical responses and by throwing their weight on the side of social, national and herd prejudices. The most popular contemporary fiction, it has been shown, unfits its readers for any novel that demands readjustment' (1979: 70). For Q. D. Leavis, then, the new commercial conditions that emerged during the Victorian era marked the tragic 'beginning of a split between popular and cultivated taste' which was, she believed, only accelerating in her own time.

As Christine Berberich observes, whilst the work of the Leavises helped create and indeed reinforce the division of literature into 'highbrow' and 'lowbrow' that still endures in some quarters to this day,

> it could, however, also be argued that the Leavises' critique of popular fiction and culture simultaneously, and seemingly incongruously, elevated its status to a subject suddenly worthy of culture and debate. Without Q. D. and F. R. Leavis, a book specifically on 'popular' literature (as compared to other literatures) might never even have seen the present day. (2015: 39)

As such, their influence on the development of the academic study of popular literature remains considerable, even if both of them found mass culture to be quite problematic in terms of what they perceived to be its harmful impact upon the intellectual faculties of the 'ordinary' reader as well as its (supposedly) detrimental wider cultural effects.

Bibliography

Arnold, Matthew [1869] (2006), *Culture and Anarchy*, Oxford: Oxford University Press.

Ayers, David (2004), *English Literature of the 1920s*, Edinburgh: Edinburgh University Press.

Berberich, Christine (2015), 'Twentieth-Century Popular: History, Theory and Context', in C. Berberich (ed.), *The Bloomsbury Introduction to Popular Fiction*, London: Bloomsbury Academic, pp. 30–52.

Docker, John (1994), 'Modernism Versus Popular Literature', in *Postmodernism and Popular Culture: A Cultural History*, Cambridge: Cambridge University Press, pp. 24–35.

Leavis, F. R. [1930] (2011), 'Mass Civilisation and Minority Culture', in *Education and the University: A Sketch for an English School*, Cambridge: Cambridge University Press, pp. 141–71.

Leavis. Q. D. [1932] (1979), *Fiction and the Reading Public*, Harmondsworth: Penguin.

Pease, Alison (2011), 'Modernism and Mass Culture', in M. Levenson (ed.), *The Cambridge Companion to Modernism*, Cambridge: Cambridge University Press, pp. 197–211.

Robertson, P. J. M. (1988), *The Leavises on Fiction*, Basingstoke: Macmillan.

Singh, G. (1995), *F. R. Leavis: A Literary Biography*, London: Duckworth.

Storey, John (2009), 'The "Culture and Civilisation" Tradition', in *Cultural Theory and Popular Culture: An Introduction*, London: Pearson and Longman, pp. 17–35.

2. The Frankfurt School

The next theoretical intervention of major relevance to the field of popular fiction studies came about due to the emergence of the so-called Frankfurt School, a group of immensely important intellectuals who were based at the Institute for Social Research in Frankfurt, Germany, between the early 1920s and the 1940s. Of particular importance here is the work of Theodor Adorno. Although his writings on 'mass culture' tended to focus specifically on radio, music, the cinema and advertising, many of the concepts he coined (both alone, and in tandem with his colleague Max Horkheimer) have become critical touchstones for scholars interested in the intellectual response to popular fiction during the twentieth century and after. As J. M. Bernstein observes,

For Adorno, the Marxist belief that capitalist forces of production will generate a free society is illusory. Capital does not possess such immediately emancipatory forces or elements; the drift of capitalist development, even the underlying or implicit drift of such development, is not towards freedom but towards further integration and domination. (Adorno 2010: 1)

'Mass culture', in the formulation of Adorno and Horkheimer, reinforces rather than challenges the status quo of this capitalist, post-industrial society.

A key plank of this theoretical approach was the idea of the so-called 'culture industry', which, as Adorno further elaborated in his 1975 essay 'The Culture Industry Reconsidered', 'transfers the profit motive naked on to cultural forms' (2010: 99), and forces together high and low culture, thereby destroying the seriousness of high art and snuffing out any potential for resistance within lower art in order to maintain social control (2010: 98). The culture industry, he continues, 'misuses its concern for the masses in order to duplicate, reinforce and strengthen their mentality, which it presumes is given and unchangeable' (2010: 99). Adorno makes it clear that he did not intend his use of the word 'industry' to be taken entirely literally, but that it instead refers to 'the standardisation of the thing itself – such as that of the Western, familiar to every movie-goer – and to the rationalisation of distribution techniques, but not strictly to the production process' (2010: 100).

In their 1944 essay (revised 1947) 'The Culture Industry: Enlightenment as Mass Deception', Adorno and Horkheimer argued that culture in its current state was characterised by homogeneity and uniformity, in part because

the people at the top are no longer so interested in concealing monopoly: as its violence becomes more open, so its power grows. Movies and radio no longer need to pretend to be art. The truth is that they are just business made into an ideology in order to justify the rubbish they deliberately produce. (2002: 1)

The ruthless process of standardisation they identified in the 'Culture Industry' is merely a precursor or parallel to the same processes on a wider societal level, such as in, for instance, politics. Categories within popular entertainment such as magazine stories are said to relate not so much to the subject matter as to classifying consumers: in their ominous phrase, 'Something is provided for all so that none may escape' (2002: 2). Paradoxically, therefore, the more choice the public appears to have within their range of mass-produced entertainment products, the less freedom he or she actually enjoys: even the varying quality provided for is really about making sure that all sectors of society, from the intellectual elite to the uneducated worker, feel that they have been catered for.

In the analysis offered here, the wide range of genres provided for by the commercial producers of popular fiction (the publishers) is in fact, largely irrelevant, in that all of these books, regardless of their ostensible differences, are actually standardised, homogenised products created by the same culture industry. Adorno and Horkheimer use the specific example of going to the cinema to see a film that we know the end of even as it begins, but they might just as well have been referring to the predictability and use of formula within popular fiction. Everything has been so carefully 'stamped with sameness' that true authenticity or art becomes impossible. The mass audience here is figured as a collective of 'helpless victims' so deceived and conditioned by the powers that be that they in fact become complicit in the system that seeks to control them. In another memorable phrase, we are told that, 'they insist upon the very ideology which enslaves them' (2002: 8). 'Leisure time' is seen as merely an extension of work intended to ready the worker for yet more thankless work. There is no real choice, only the seductive illusion of choice, and 'a constant reproduction of the same thing' (2002: 8).

In his essay 'The Schema of Mass Culture' (1991), Adorno further outlined what he saw as the true nature of the culture industry, which results in the replacement of imagination by a 'mechanically relentless control mechanism', erodes real conflict, and has the 'ritual conclusion' of the happy ending (2010: 64). In relation to popular fiction, he observes of the

> socio critical novels which are fed though the bestseller mechanism, we can no longer distinguish how far the horrors narrated in them serve the denunciation of society as opposed to the amusement of those who do not yet have the Roman circuses they are really waiting for. (2010: 68)

Mass culture is pre-determined, pre-patterned and pre-digested; and people willingly go along with it because they know that it provides the 'mores they will surely need as their passport to a monopolised life' (2010: 92). 'The Schema of Mass Culture' concludes with a typically dystopian assertion that mass culture potentially even possesses the means to help create the conditions in which fascism may flourish; in part because it dehumanises people through a process known as 'reification', which imposes signs from above, and not from within or below – and is essentially, according to this reading, a nightmare that we all willingly participate in (2010: 95). However, it is also important, as Ross Wilson observes, to bear in mind that Adorno does not necessarily see cultural products as being bad in and of themselves. Instead, 'What Adorno objects to in contemporary culture is precisely the failure of cultural products to fulfil their own potential. That failure is a consequence of the fact that potential is sacrificed because everything must be fit into existing moulds' (Wilson 2007: 42).

As John Storey (2009) notes, the work of Adorno's fellow Frankfurt School thinker Walter Benjamin, and in particular, his famous 1936 essay 'The Work of Art in an Age of Mechanical Reproduction', provides a more hopeful reading of the masses not as passive consumers, but as individuals with the capacity to actively engage with and appropriate mass culture for personal, political and even potentially subversive ends. Though he was also mainly discussing film, photography and art, Benjamin observed that mass literacy and advanced print culture had brought about a massive transformation in the relationship between writer and reader, and even suggested that the distinction between author and public was about to lose its basic character (1999: 225). Even though he was obviously writing long before the advent of the digital age, Benjamin's discussion of the ways in which technological advances can transform not just our relationship with art, but cultural products in general, is still immensely relevant.

Bibliography

Adorno, Theodor W. [1991] (2010), 'The Schema of Mass Culture', in *The Culture Industry: Essays on Mass Culture*, London: Routledge, pp. 61–98.

Adorno, Theodor W. [1975] (2010), 'The Culture Industry Reconsidered', in *The Culture Industry: Essays on Mass Culture*, London: Routledge, pp. 98–107.

Adorno, Theodor W. and Max Horkheimer [1944] (2002), 'The Culture Industry: Enlightenment as Mass Deception', in *Dialectic of Enlightenment: Philosophical Fragments*, Stanford: Stanford University Press, pp. 94–136.

Benjamin, Walter [1936] (1999), 'The Work of Art in an Age of Mechanical Reproduction', in *Illuminations*, London: Pimlico, 1999, pp. 211–14.

Storey, John (2009), 'The Frankfurt School', in *Cultural Theory and Popular Culture: An Introduction*, London: Pearson and Longman, pp. 62–70.

Wilson, Ross (2007), *Theodor Adorno: Routledge Critical Thinkers*, London: Routledge.

3. Structuralism and Popular Fiction

The structuralist fascination with the underlying organisation of texts has meant that popular fiction, often considered to be a particularly formulaic, predictable form of literature, has for many critics represented an attractive and indeed obvious subject for this kind of scrutiny. From the mid-twentieth century onwards, critics began applying theoretical insights derived from the structuralist approach to language and reality to culture at large. For instance, French anthropologist Claude Levi-Strauss used structuralist methods to analyse the rituals, taboos and myths of 'primitive' cultures. Another leading French theorist, Roland Barthes, applied the structuralist method to 1950s French culture in his essay collection *Mythologies* (1957), in order to tease out the hidden assumptions and ideological structures which he saw as underlining (and indeed, creating) our perceptions of the world.

One of the most famous early structuralist readings of a popular fiction narrative is Italian author and critic Umberto Eco's analysis of the James Bond novels in his 1965 essay 'Narrative Structures in Fleming'. In it, he describes the way in which the first novel in the series, *Casino Royale* (1953), establishes 'all the elements for the building a machine that functions basically on a set of precise units governed by rigorous combinational rules' (Eco 1965: 159). Eco broke the novel down into nine specific 'moves' arranged according to a 'perfectly pre-arranged scheme', arguing that although there were often inversions and variations in the novels that followed, the same basic elements were present in every novel, albeit not necessarily in the same order every time. Eco would later write on 'The Myth of Superman' (1972), in which the Man of Steel's relationship to his mythological predecessors was discussed alongside an astute analysis of the narrative structure of the typical Superman comic. In the essay collection, *The Sign of Three: Dupin, Holmes, Pierce* (1983), which Eco edited along with Thomas A. Sebeok, contributors detailed undertook semiotic readings of classic crime fiction, and in doing so, provided an even more detailed reading of the 'system of signs' they saw as underpinning a specific popular genre.

The collection also provides further evidence that crime is probably the genre that has been examined most often (and certainly most famously) from a structuralist perspective. The intellectual 'puzzle' aspect of 'Golden Age' (1920s–1950s) detective fiction had indeed rendered the genre a semi-respectable subject of scholarly inquiry long before horror, romance or science fiction texts made their way onto university reading lists. The seemingly clear-cut nature of the genre's basic narrative structure – a crime is committed and then investigated – also makes it a particularly attractive subject for this kind of formalist analysis. Leading structuralist critic Tzvetan Todorov even outlined an influential 'Typology of Detective Fiction' in his book *The Poetics of Prose* (1966; 1977, in translation). Drawing upon the work of the Russian formalists, Todorov argued that there were three specific types of detective fiction: the thriller, the whodunit and the suspense story (he also saw the thriller as being a kind of detective story). Todorov believed that each detective story can in fact be understood as two specific stories, the 'whodunit' and 'the investigation', but that depending on which sub-type one is dealing with, these elements are rearranged. As Todorov's findings underlined, the structuralist approach can be particularly useful for critics looking to draw broad conclusions about a particular genre. It is for this reason that in the two most important critical studies to date of the romance genre, Janice A. Radway's *Reading the Romance* (1984) and Pamela Regis's *A Natural History of the Romance* (1996), we can see strong traces of the structuralist influence in the chapters in which each author seeks to define the specific narrative structures of the genre.

Based as it is on a quasi-scientific methodology (diagrams, charts and tables of various sorts are not at all uncommon in structuralist readings), structuralism was also attractive to critics during the early years of popular fiction studies, because the approach provides such an obviously rational, methodical framework for approaching 'non-canonical' texts. Whilst it has long since been supplemented by a wide range of alternative theoretical approaches, structuralism therefore still furnishes a useful theoretical footing for critics who intend to embark upon an in-depth analysis of formulaic elements pertaining to a genre, or an individual work of fiction, as well as those considering an individual text or author's relationship to wider generic and societal structures.

Bibliography

Barthes, Roland [1957] (2009), *Mythologies*, London: Vintage.
Eco, Umberto (1972), 'The Myth of Superman', *Diacritics*, vol. 2, no. 1 (Spring), pp. 14–22.

Eco, Umberto [1965] (1984), 'Narrative Structures in Fleming', in *The Role of the Reader: Explorations in the Semiotics of Texts*, Bloomington: Indiana University Press, pp. 144–75.

Hawkes, Terence [1977] (2003), *Structuralism and Semiotics*, London: Routledge.

McCracken, Scott (1998), 'Detective Fiction', in *Pulp: Reading Popular Fiction*, Manchester: Manchester University Press, pp. 50–74.

Radway, Janice A. (1984), *Reading the Romance: A Natural History of the Romance Novel*, Chapel Hill: University of North Carolina Press.

Regis, Pamela [1996] (2002), *A Natural History of the Romance Novel*, Philadelphia: University of Pennsylvania Press.

Todorov, Tzvetan [1966] (1977), 'The Typology of Detective Fiction', in *The Poetics of Prose*, Ithaca, NY: Cornell University Press, pp. 42–52.

4. The Sociological Approach: Marxism, Cultural Materialism and Cultural Studies

Sociological approaches to literature are grounded in the conviction that the most insightful means of analysing a text is to consider it in relation to the economic, social, political and cultural contexts from which it has emerged. Because popular fiction has always been associated with issues of commercial production, distribution and mass appeal (even though to suggest that texts which have been categorised as 'literary' as opposed to 'popular' are somehow magically protected from these kinds of influences would be entirely inaccurate), it is hardly surprising that theoretical approaches to popular texts are often rooted in this perspective. As the work of the Frankfurt School underlined, narratives considered to be products of what some critics call 'mass culture' lend themselves particularly well to modes of analysis focusing on the links between popular culture, economics, political ideology and social control. The theoretical approach taken by Adorno, Horkheimer, Marcuse and Benjamin owed a great deal to Marxism, and indeed, many of their most useful concepts and critical terms were directly derived from the work of Marx and Engels. As is the case with the sociological approach more generally, however, although there are many important critiques of popular *culture* influenced by this theoretical perspective, popular *fiction* specifically is not a particularly common focal point, unless it is within the context of discussion of certain key genres, as we shall see. Indeed, Marxism is mentioned only in passing in all of the most significant introductions and companions to popular fiction published since the late 1990s, and even then, it is almost always cited in relation to its influence upon the Frankfurt School.

One of the few specific considerations of the relationship between Marxist theory and popular fiction is Tony Bennett's 1981 essay 'Marxism and Popular Fiction'. Bennett (who also includes film and TV in his definition of 'popular fiction') argues that popular fiction is defined within literary criticism as being that which is 'not literature' and so is therefore conceptualised in negative terms (in relation to what it is *not*, rather than what it *is*). He suggests that the Marxist neglect of popular fiction is indicative of a more general weakness within the Marxist literary project, and claims that Marxist critics, with the expectation of the Frankfurt School and the key cultural studies figure Raymond Williams (who we will come to in a moment), have replicated the value-based canonical judgements inherent in 'bourgeois' criticism, thereby duplicating its assumptions and exclusions (2003: 241).

Some popular genres have, however, been usefully looked at from a Marxist perspective, with one of the most frequent being science fiction. As neo-Marxist critic Frederic Jameson has argued, the desire to change or to challenge the status quo is a central tenet of Marxism, whilst the SF genre has the imaginative scope to conjure up empirically grounded alternatives to society as we find it today (Tally 2013: 35). The Marxist approach remains an important one in SF criticism to this day, as chapters in the likes of *The Cambridge Companion to Science Fiction* (2003) and *Red Planets: Marxism and Science Fiction* (2009) underline.

Marxist economist Ernest Mandel's *Delightful Murder: A Social History of the Crime Story* (1984) attempted to contextualise the emergence and development of the crime genre as a response to the wider structural changes in the organisation of 'bourgeois' society. In a response to anyone who might find it 'frivolous' for a Marxist to analyse popular fiction, Mandel persuasively countered by arguing that historical materialism should be applied to all social phenomena, and that none was by nature less worthy of study than others (1984: viii). Gothic studies has been influenced by insights derived from Jacques Derrida's *Specters of Marx* (1994), which helped give rise to the critical arena of 'hauntology', which is influenced by the fact that Marx often deployed a distinctly 'gothic' vocabulary of 'ghosts, vampires and walking corpses' in his writing (Warwick 2013: 372).

Marxist analysis was a major influence on the theoretical approach to mass culture formulated by the so-called 'cultural materialists'. The work of British academic Raymond Williams is of considerable significance here. Within cultural materialism, history is seen as a matter of subjective interpretation rather than eternal fact, and it is argued that special attention needs to be paid to overlooked, marginalised and suppressed voices within a particular culture (Makaryk 1993: 23). Along with Richard Hoggart, E. P. Thompson, Stuart Hall and Paddy Whannel, Williams was a key figure both in the development of cultural studies as a distinct area of academic interest in the UK, and in the creation of the Centre for Contemporary Cultural Studies at the University of Birmingham, established in 1964 (hence the term, 'The Birmingham School'). Williams's take on the relationship between literary fiction and popular fiction is usefully outlined by Jon Thompson (1993). He observes that Williams's wider critique of traditional positions pertaining to the supposed divide between 'high' and 'low' culture means that definitions of what does and does not constitute 'literature' are relative, subjective positions, and that the exclusion of popular fiction from the canon based on such assumptions is a function of ideology rather than any kind of fixed truth (1993: 80). In other words, the kind of rigid barrier between 'high' and 'low' culture favoured by the likes of the Leavises is no longer seen as feasible or appropriate.

One of the most significant publications to emerge from those associated with the Birmingham School from a popular fiction perspective was *The Popular Arts* (1964) by Stuart Hall and Paddy Whannel, which included chapters on Raymond Chandler, Micky Spillane and Ian Fleming, as well as sections on the thriller and romance fiction. Hall and Whannel distinguished between what they called 'popular art', which they said 'exists through the medium of a personal style' and they saw as a positive manifestation of culture created by and for the people, and 'mass art', which 'often destroys all trace of individuation and idiosyncrasy which makes a work compelling and living, and assumes a sort of de-personalised quality, a no-style' (1966: 68). For instance, in an assertion that recalls similar opinions expressed by Q. D. Leavis, the contemporary romance novel is here associated with the danger 'not that they make us feel too strongly and deeply, but that they confine our very notions of love within their conventional framework, and thus prevent us from feeling strongly and deeply enough' (1966: 195).

Because their book was also intended as a practical guide for the teaching of popular culture, the authors advocated training young people in the kind of subtle 'discrimination' that would allow them to differentiate between 'popular art' and this formulaic and 'machine produced' mass art (1966: 37). As Daniel Horowitz notes however, whilst Hall and Whannel draw from Matthew Arnold and the Leavises 'a commitment to use discrimination and judgement in order to ana- lyse popular culture [. . .] in their hands, discrimination was not, as it was for the Leavisites, a tool to criticise debased popular culture, but rather to challenge the widely accepted boundaries of high/low and good/bad that dominated the discussion of culture' (2012: 261–2). *The Popular Arts* therefore remains one of the most significant early attempts to outline a distinct pedagogical approach to the critical study and evaluation of popular culture, including popular fiction.

Another theorist whose insights into the material aspects and social conditions of popular culture were informed by Marxism was the French sociologist Pierre Bourdieu, whose consideration of the relationship between cultural preferences (or 'taste') and social class remains significant. Bourdieu's formulation of terms such as 'field', 'habitus' and his notion of so-called 'Cultural Capital' (the form of acquired knowledge which comes from the education we receive within our family, as well as the wider social and institutional educa- tion which permits us to appreciate and engage with specific cultural products) was extremely influential. In *Distinction: A Social Critique of the Judgement of Taste* (1977), Bourdieu outlined the multitude of social factors that play their part in informing the aesthetic and cultural tastes of the individual. As he put it, 'taste classifies, and it classifies the classifier' (1999: 6). As Scott McCracken notes in his dis- cussion of Bourdieu's significance to the study of popular fiction, this focus upon the consumer is important because it suggests that the way in which we read popular fiction is a result of our social circumstances (including our gender and class) and also posits that new kinds of taste can be produced by new social classes (1998: 38).

Bibliography

Bennett, Tony [1981] (2003), 'Marxism and Popular Fiction', in P. Humm, P. Stigant and P. Widdowson (eds), *Popular Fictions: Essays in Literature and History*, London: Routledge, pp. 237–65.
Bourdieu, Pierre (1999), *Distinction: A Social Critique on the Judgement of Taste*, London: Routledge.

Fowler, Bridget (1977), 'Bourdieu, the Popular and the Periphery', in *Pierre Bourdieu and Critical Theory: Critical Investigations*, London: Sage, pp. 160–73.

Hall, Stuart and Paddy Whannel (1964), *The Popular Arts*, London: Hutchinson Educational, pp. 142–64.

Horowitz, Daniel (2012), *Consuming Pleasures: Intellectuals and Popular Culture in the Post War World*, Philadelphia: University of Pennsylvania Press.

Johnson, Randal (1993), 'Introduction' to P. Bourdieu, *The Field of Cultural Production: Essays on Art and Literature*, Cambridge: Polity Press, pp. 1–28.

McCracken, Scott (1998), *Pulp: Reading Popular Fiction*, Manchester and New York: Manchester University Press.

Makaryk, Rima Irene (ed.) (1993), *Encyclopaedia of Contemporary Literary Theory: Approaches, Scholars, Terms*, Toronto: University of Toronto Press.

Mandel, Ernest (1984), *Delightful Murder: A Social History of the Crime Story*, London: Pluto Press.

Tally, Robert T. Jr (2013), *Utopia in the Age of Globalization: Space, Representation, and the World System*, New York: Palgrave Macmillan.

Thompson, Jon (1993), 'Realisms and Modernisms: Raymond Williams and Popular Fiction', in D. L. Dworkin and L. G. Roman, *Views beyond the Border Country: Raymond Williams and Cultural Politics*, New York and London: Routledge, pp. 72–91.

Warwick, Alexandra (2013), 'Ghosts, Monsters and Spirits, 1840–1900', in G. Byron and D. Townshend (eds), *The Gothic World*, London: Routledge, pp. 366–75.

Williams, Raymond [1977] (2009), *Marxism and Literature*, Oxford: Oxford University Press.

5. Reader-response Criticism

In contrast to liberal humanism, the reader-response approach to literature rejects the idea that texts contain certain inviolable, enduring, fixed meanings transmitted to an inherently passive reader. Neither are the intentions of the author or the form and content of the text considered the sole repositories of meaning. On the contrary, meaning is seen as being created by the reader as he or she engages with the text.

The reader-response approach has been useful within popular fiction studies because it has allowed critics to engage with issues of readership and gender in particular in a very direct way. In fact, one of the most well-known reader-response studies is an analysis of the way in which a small group of readers engaged with a popular genre: Janice A. Radway's *Reading the Romance* (1984). Radway's approach was informed by the ethnographic approach (a methodology she derived from anthropology). She undertook an empiric investigation of popular reading habits, focusing in particular upon the 'social event' of reading. She did this by investigating the preferences and attitudes of a small group of women in the Midwestern community of 'Smithton', all of whom interacted on a regular basis with the local bookstore proprietor, 'Dot', whose recommendations and opinions of particular romance novels and authors were highly influential within this circle.

Radway, a feminist critic who began the study with (as she later admitted) some major reservations about what she initially perceived to be the inherently problematic nature of the romance genre, was particularly interested in exploring the intimate relationship between these women and the novels that they were reading. Her discussion sessions with this small group of romance fans led her to the conclusion that, amongst other things, the genre functioned as an invaluable 'compensatory' literature for middle-class wives and mothers, supplying them with emotional release that would otherwise have been denied them in the course of their everyday lives, because their proscribed social roles left them little room for 'guiltless, self-interested pursuit of individual pleasure' (1984: 95).

Radway's discussions with the Smithton women also informed her construction of a structuralist outline of what they considered to be the narrative elements of the 'ideal romance'. As Radway acknowledged at the time, the small nature of her sample group meant that her argument could only be applied with caution to the genre as a whole, whilst some later critics (in particular Pamela Regis) have also argued that the conclusions derived from her textual analysis were flawed because they were confined to one particular sub-genre only (the historical romance) and a limited number of authors. Radway herself later critiqued what she characterised as some of her own biases regarding the appeal and effect of the kind of 'reading for pleasure' in which her subjects engaged. Nevertheless, *Reading the Romance* remains a landmark study in reader-response criticism (as well as popular fiction studies generally) not least for focusing academic attention upon both a genre and a group of readers that had largely been overlooked until that point.

More recent exercises in reader-response criticism related to popular fiction, almost all of which reference Radway's influence, have been particularly useful for exploring the ways in which actual reader interpretations and interactions with texts complicate the assumptions of authors, academics and the media. There have, for instance, been several analyses of the Harry Potter phenomenon from this perspective, and the approach frequently comes up in critical discussions of the *Twilight* series. More recently, E. L. James's *Fifty Shades of Grey* series (2011–12) has also been the subject of reader-response analysis (Deller 2013). The academic study of fanfiction, itself a form of popular fiction that has its direct roots in fan responses to a particular text, also often draws upon the reader-response approach.

Bibliography

Deller, Ruth (2013), 'Reading the BDSM Romance: Reader Responses to *Fifty Shades*', *Sexualities*, vol. 16, no. 8 (December), pp. 932–50.

Holub, Robert C. (1984), *Reception Theory: A Critical Introduction*, London: Routledge.

Radway, Janice A. [1984] (1987), *Reading the Romance*, London: Verso.

Radway, Janice A. (1994), 'Romance and the Work of Fantasy: Struggles over Feminine Sexuality and Subjectivity at Century's End', in J. Vruz and J. Lewis (eds), *Viewing, Reading, Listening: Audiences and Cultural Reception*, Boulder: Westview Press, pp. 213–31.

Regis, Pamela (2003), *A Natural History of the Romance Genre*, Philadelphia: University of Pennsylvania Press.

Storey, John (2010), 'Feminism and Romance Reading', in *Cultural Studies and the Study of Popular Culture*, Edinburgh: Edinburgh University Press, pp. 66–76.

6. Postmodernism and Popular Fiction

The emergence of postmodernism as a theoretical movement is generally linked to an increasing resistance towards the often rigid divisions between high and low culture that were often held to be a central tenet of modernism. Indeed, John Carey (in his 1992 book *The Intellectuals and the Masses*) has argued that a frequently horrified response to 'mass culture' (and to 'the masses' themselves) was a central feature of the modernist project in England in particular, as was a tendency to see 'mass culture', the supposedly 'debased' products of what Adorno and Horkheimer would characterise as the 'culture industry' as degraded and *degrading* artefacts that represented a dangerous and even anti-democratic form of 'levelling down'. This line of thought can be detected in Q. D. and F. R. Leavis, as we have seen, but also in the post-war cultural criticism of US critic Dwight Macdonald, whose 1960 essay on the intertwined phenomena he referred to as 'Masscult and Midcult' took a similarly dim view of the forms of popular culture he considered so bad that they were not so much 'non art' as 'anti-art' (2011: 4). Echoes of this distrust of the 'popular' can also be detected in the work of more recent cultural commentators such as Curtis White (*The Middle Mind: Why Americans Don't Think for Themselves*, 2004) and Chris Hedges, who embarks upon a particularly lacerating take on contemporary American culture in *Empire of Illusion: The End of Literacy and the Triumph of Spectacle* (2014).

As John Storey suggests, 'the postmodernism of the late 1950s and 60s was therefore a populist attack on the elitism of modernism. It signalled a refusal of what Andreas Huyssen (1986) calls "the great divide [. . .] [a] discourse which insists on the categorical distinction between high art and mass culture"' (2009: 183). Postmodernism, as Jean-François Lyotard famously put it in *The Postmodern Condition: A Report on Knowledge* (1979) is said to bring about a crisis in the status of knowledge, and, according to his analysis, is defined by its 'incredulity towards metanarratives' – with the 'metanarrative' being the broad frameworks that we use to tell the stories – political, cultural, ideological – which allow us to understand and structure reality. According to postmodernist theorists, there are no certain, inviolable truths, and the inherent artificiality and uncertainty of the stories that we tell ourselves is a given. One of the most significant early discussions of the relationship between postmodernism and popular fiction was American literary critic Leslie Fiedler's 1969 essay 'Cross the Border – Close the Gap'. In it, he presciently suggested that the emerging postmodernist tendency in American literature would provide a means of 'closing the gap' between high and low culture that had been reinforced by modernism. Fiedler saw the continuation of what he considered to be outmoded high-modernist distinctions between 'High Art' and 'Mass Art' as a manifestation of 'concealed class bias', and argued that 'Pop Art' – including that which we would now call 'popular fiction' – was inherently political, and inherently subversive, because it threatened all boundaries (1969: 287).

As Linda Hutcheon notes, Fiedler also argued that postmodernism crossed boundaries – or 'closed gaps' – by ironising both high and low culture (she gives the example of the mixing of religious history and detective fiction in Umberto Eco's 1980 bestseller *The Name of the Rose*) or by using familiar genre tropes in sophisticated ways, or in parodic and metafictional forms (1988: 44). A good example of this tendency can also be seen in Mark Z. Danielewski's *House of Leaves* (2000), a haunted house novel that uses tropes and basic plot elements seen in countless other supernatural horror stories, but is also, simultaneously (and typically for a postmodernist text), a witty and typographically inventive commentary on the nature of fiction and reality. This is exactly the kind of epistemological uncertainty that thrives in the postmodern text. As Hutcheon puts it, 'Postmodernism is both academic and popular, elitist and accessible' (1988: 44). Indeed, it has been suggested that increased academic interest in popular culture – including popular fiction – is itself representative of the kind of erosion of traditional markers of cultural value associated with postmodern thought.

The popular genre that has to date been most associated with postmodernism is probably science fiction. As Bran Nicol has argued, 'its potential to offer an alternative to realism' has itself proved central to postmodernist thinking (2009: 164). Whilst Nicol argues that the cyberpunk sub-genre is the most postmodern variety of SF, the genre is also central to the postmodernist speculations of Fredric Jameson, who uses a novel by Philip K. Dick as a starting point for his well-known discussion of nostalgia in an essay featured in *Postmodernism: Or, the Cultural Logic of Late Capitalism* (1991). Popular fiction, for Jameson, is part of what he characterises as the 'paraliterature' that has arisen from the erosion of the 'high-modernist frontier' between high culture and commercial culture, a 'degraded landscape of schlock and kitsch' that fascinates postmodernists for this very reason (1991: 2).

One of the most interesting recent critical discussions regarding the interplay between postmodernism and popular fiction specifically (as opposed to the *many* postmodernist discussions related to popular culture more generally, which tend to exclude genre fiction entirely) is that revolving round what has become known as the 'genrefication' debate. The debate was sparked by the publication in 2012 of Arthur Krystal's essay 'Easy Writers: Guilty Pleasures without Guilt' in *The New Yorker*, in which he argued that in comparison to the clear boundaries between literary and genre fiction of a previous age, 'the literary climate has changed: the canon has been impeached, formerly neglected writers have been saluted, and the presumed superiority of one type of book over another no longer passes unquestioned' (2012: online). Krystal's piece aroused a great deal of critical attention, in part because he had highlighted a trend that had been becoming increasingly obvious: that younger American writers in particular seem increasingly happy to subvert or circumvent entirely the old barriers between genre and 'literary' or 'serious' fiction.

Responding to Krystal's comments, fellow critic Lev Grossman (himself the author of a well-received metafictional fantasy novel, *The Magicians*, 2009), argued that genre fiction was prominent at the moment due to more than the often-cited need for simple escapism. Reciting a long list of writers associated with literary fiction who have been borrowing from genre fiction of late, he argued that whilst we expect literary revolutions to come from above, from 'the difficult, the high end, the densely written [. . .] I don't think that's what's going on. Instead we're getting a revolution from below, coming up from the supermarket aisles. Genre fiction is the technology that will disrupt the literary novel as we know it' (2012: online). In similar terms, Joshua Rothman – who came up with the term 'genrefication' in the first place – later suggested that we might be 'headed for a total collapse of the genre system' – a 'genre apocalypse', in which, as Fiedler suggested a generation ago, the old boundaries were no longer appropriate, or indeed, applicable (2014: online). Therefore, one of the central characteristics of postmodernist thought appears to have anticipated the on-going evolution in the relationship between the 'literary' and the 'popular'. Indeed, Tim Lanzendörfer argues that, 'The novel is increasingly headed towards amalgamated forms that combine traditional realist forms – the bildungsroman, the social novel, the historical novel – with formal elements previously confined to the popular genres of science fiction, crime and fantasy, among others' (2016: 3). It seems increasingly likely that he will be proved correct.

Bibliography

Connor, Stephen (1990), *Postmodernist Culture: An Introduction to Theories of the Popular*, Oxford: Basil Blackwell.

Fiedler, Leslie [1969] (1975), 'Cross the Border – Close the Gap', in *A New Fiedler Reader*, New York: Prometheus Books, pp. 270–94.

Grossman, Lev (2012), 'Literary Revolution in the Supermarket Aisle: Genre Fiction is Disruptive Technology', *Time*, 23 May [online].

Hutcheon, Linda (1988), *A Poetics of Postmodernism: History, Theory, Fiction*, London: Routledge.

Jameson, Fredric (1991), *Postmodernism: Or, the Cultural Logic of Late Capitalism*, Durham, NC: Duke University Press.

Krystal, Arthur (2012), 'Easy Writers: Guilty Pleasures without Guilt', *The New Yorker*, 28 May [online].

Lanzendörfer, Tim (ed.) (2016), *The Poetics of Genre in the Contemporary Novel*, Lanham, MD: Lexington Books.

Macdonald, Dwight (2011), *Masscult and Midcult: Essays against the American Grain*, ed. J. Summers, New York: New York Review of Books.

Nicol, Bran (2009), 'Two Postmodern Genres: Cyberpunk and "Metaphysical" Detective Fiction', in *The Cambridge Introduction to Postmodern Fiction*, Cambridge: Cambridge University Press, pp. 164–84.

Rothman, Joshua (2014), 'A Better Way to Think about the Genre Debate', *The New Yorker*, 6 November [online].

Storey, John (2009), 'Postmodernism', in *Cultural Theory and Popular Culture: An Introduction*, Essex: Pearson Educational, pp. 187–217.

7. Race, Globalisation and Popular Fiction

Just as the long overdue turn towards issues of gender and sexuality pioneered by feminist critics from the 1980s onwards heralded a major shift of focus within literary and cultural studies in general, so too is it likely (and necessary) that future developments regarding the academic investigation of popular fiction will involve an increasing emphasis upon the representation and interrogation of issues related to race, nationality and ethnicity. There is also much scope for further study into the way in which specific generic archetypes and tropes originating from a Western context have been adapted and transformed by authors and readers who originate from outside these cultural and geographical contexts, as well as the ways in which Western authors appropriate and reconfigure concepts adopted from outside their own cultural context.

There has been an inherent bias towards the discussion of works by white, English-speaking authors within popular fiction studies to date. The long-standing commercial dominance of British and American publishing conglomerates and booksellers means that novels and stories first published in the English language have a higher global profile and wider distribution pattern than those initially written in other languages. In addition, as any introduction to popular fiction has to acknowledge, all of the major popular genres have their principal roots in forms of writing in English that emerged during the eighteenth and nineteenth centuries. It is also worth noting that almost all of the major existing works on popular fiction as a *general* subject area (as opposed to works dedicated to specific popular genres or sub-genres) have been written by academics associated with the British university system in particular. This in part reflects the fact that the strong cultural studies tradition established in the UK during the 1960s played a considerable role in focusing academic attention there on all forms of popular culture, including popular fiction, before it had gained a firm foothold elsewhere.

Academics from an Anglocentric and North American background also have a tendency to focus upon popular texts that have emerged from within a publishing tradition and a historical context with which they are already acquainted. A similar tendency to focus upon that which is culturally 'familiar' has also informed the study of eighteenth- and nineteenth-century North American popular fiction. Even very recent overviews of popular fiction tend to mention non-British and non-American texts only in passing. Indeed, because it is intended to provide a representative introduction to the state of contemporary popular fiction, the book you are reading right now is no different. This bias, whilst perhaps understandable to an extent for practical reasons to do with the origins and evolution of popular fiction, does mean that the opportunities to engage with pre-existing and emerging genre fiction from the non-English speaking (and non-Western) world in particular are often overlooked. As has become troublingly apparent in recent years, the publishing world is still an overwhelmingly white and Anglophone one, which means that publishing opportunities for aspiring genre authors whose fiction is not deemed sufficiently 'commercial' have also been somewhat curtailed.

The one major exception in recent years has been the substantial amount of media and academic attention paid to the so-called 'Nordic Noir' phenomenon. However, whilst these novels were initially published in languages other than English, they still involve predominately white protagonists, and are, by their very nature, obviously Eurocentric. Within the subject areas related to specific popular genres, there has been, however, more of an effort to acknowledge and engage with racial, ethnic and geographical diversity. For instance, the 'Global Gothic' initiative (which originated at Stirling University, Scotland) is intended to help focus critical attention upon horror and gothic texts and traditions from around the world, in order to help broaden the traditional focus upon European and North American authors and texts only. Similarly, 'The International Crime Fiction Research Group' based at Queen's University, Belfast, centres on issues of transnational circulation and cross-cultural exchange particular to that genre.

Because science fiction so often dramatises anxieties related to the depiction of the 'alien' other, hybridity and imperialism, it lends itself particularly well to critical inquiry informed by postcolonial theories and perspectives. Recent examples in this vein include Jessica Langer's *Postcolonialism and Science Fiction* (2012) and John Rieder's *Colonialism and the Emergence of Science Fiction* (2008). In addition, Helen Young has recently used the fantasy genre as a 'microcosm of popular culture to investigate the discourses around race and racial difference which circulate in the Anglophone world' (2016: 1). Langer notes that science fiction written in non-English languages has tended to be marginalised by the global publishing industry (and, as noted above, the same is arguably true of popular fiction in general), as has work by writers of colour and writers from 'post-colonial' backgrounds.

It's an insight that highlights one of the paradoxes of an increasingly globalised 'culture industry'. On the one hand, cheaper, faster publishing techniques, wider distribution, and in particular, the transformations that digital publishing has wrought upon the industry in the past decade should, in theory, lead to more diversity and much greater access and opportunity for authors of all national, racial and geographical backgrounds. However, just as the emergence of the global blockbuster on cinema screens has led to accusations of increasing blandness and homogeneity, so is there the danger that instant access to European and American popular fiction will have the consequence of pushing distinctively 'home-gown' genre fiction even further towards the periphery of wider cultural visibility.

Yet, as the work of academics working within a range of areas also highlights, popular fiction manifests itself in many fascinating and telling ways around the world. Specific types of popular fiction may originate within particular national contexts (for instance, Japan invented both Manga and the so-called 'Light' novel), or specific racial and ethnic contexts (as is the case with the genre known as 'Street Lit', which is particularly associated with African American authors and readers). In addition, genres that may seem quite familiar from a British or North American perspective have rich histories elsewhere in the world that are only just beginning to be academically explored. For instance, there is a whole parallel pop culture history of the Cold War to be found in the many science fiction novels from the Soviet

Union and Eastern Europe published between the introduction of Communism and the collapse of the Iron Curtain. Thanks to the recent success of 2015 Hugo Award winner *The Three-Body Problem* by Liu Cixin (2008: released in English translation in 2014), Chinese SF is only now appearing on the publishing radar in the West. Just as worthwhile are examinations of how genres associated with the West have been appropriated by non-Western writers. India has had a thriving comics scene since the 1980s, with titles that often feature home-grown superheroes who combine aspects of both Hindu mythology with more familiar (to Western eyes) genre tropes. There is also a large readership for a distinctively Indian variety of 'Chick-Lit' novels focusing on young, urban professionals.

Aside from the need to examine distinctive national varieties and adaptations of popular genres, scholars within popular fiction studies are also becoming increasingly conscious of issues pertaining to racial and ethnic representation. For instance, as the extensive media coverage surrounding the debut of the Pakistani-American (and proudly Muslim) Marvel comics superheroine 'Ms. Marvel' in 2013 demonstrates, genre fiction in all of its modes and formats is still dominated by white authors and white protagonists, to the extent that a break-out star such as Kamala Khan becomes of even greater significance to readers who might otherwise have felt excluded from mainstream media representation. Social media campaigns such as the US-based 'We Need Diverse Books' movement, which began by calling for greater diversity within children's and young adult books and soon attracted a great deal of supportive media coverage and online-commentary, also emphasise the growing online clamour for publishers to engage with a more diverse and racially inclusive range of readers and authors. Whilst, as previously noted, the tendency to focus predominately upon English-speaking, white, and British and American authored texts does undoubtedly owe much to the historical development of popular fiction, it is obvious that one of the subject's major growth areas involves the need for around a more nuanced, representative consideration of issues pertaining to race, ethnicity and nationality.

Bibliography

Byron, Glennis (ed.) (2013), *Global Gothic*, Manchester: Manchester University Press.

Langer, Jessica (2012), *Post-Colonialism and Science Fiction*, Basingstoke: Palgrave Macmillan.

Storey, John (1996), 'Globalisation and Popular Culture', in *Cultural Studies and the Study of Popular Culture*, Edinburgh: Edinburgh University Press, pp. 160–72.

Young, Helen (2016), *Race and Popular Fantasy Literature: Habits of Whiteness*, New York: Routledge.

The International Crime Fiction Research Group: <http://international-crimefiction.org/about-2/> (last accessed 15 April 2016)

We Need Diverse Books: <http://weneeddiversebooks.tumblr.com/> (last accessed 15 April 2016)

Ken Liu, 'China Dreams: Contemporary Chinese Science Fiction' <http://clarkesworldmagazine.com/liu_12_14/> (last accessed 15 April 2016)

8. Feminism, Sexuality and Gender Studies

The emergence of a distinctly feminist approach to literature in general (and therefore popular fiction specifically) is directly related to the establishment of the modern women's rights movement in the 1960s and 1970s. Feminist activists and theorists were acutely conscious of the relationship between the mass media and the perpetuation of restrictive ideas about gender roles and 'appropriate' modes of behaviour for both men and women (Rich 2007). For instance, Betty Friedan devoted a chapter of *The Feminine Mystique* (1963) to an interrogation of the way in which popular women's magazines of the 1950s allegedly promoted a repressive domestic ideology through their consistent reproduction of the image of the 'Happy Housewife Heroine' in articles, advertisements and popular fiction. One important early discussion of popular fiction from an explicitly feminist perspective came in the 1972 essay 'What Can a Heroine Do? Or Why Women Can't Write', in which author and critic Joanna Russ argued that there were very few stories in which women were protagonists, because women were always perceived from a male perspective. 'Our literature is not about women. It is not about women and men equally. It is by and about men' (1995: 81). Even when women did appear, she stated, they existed only in relation to the male protagonist, or were reduced to a small number of crude character types, which only reinforced the social roles that they were supposed to play. Russ then went on to suggest that three specific types of genre fiction – the 'whodunit', supernatural fiction and her own favourite genre as a writer, science fiction – could present the possibility of an escape from the 'Culture

= Male' equation because they utilised plots that were not limited to one sex, because the sex of the protagonist was irrelevant. Russ's later essay, 'Somebody's Trying to Kill Me and I Think it's My Husband' (1973), on the so-called 'Modern Gothics' – mass market romances featuring plots in which virginal heroines were drawn to dangerous, but charismatic older men – combined witty structuralist analysis with astute social critique.

Given that romance fiction was (and remains) the popular genre most associated with female writers and authors, a tendency which many critics claim helps account for the fact that the genre was largely ignored by academia until the rise of feminist criticism in the 1970s and 1980s, it is hardly surprising that several of the most significant feminist studies of popular fiction deal specifically with the romance. For some feminist theorists the romance was even seen as a deeply problematic form of writing that perpetuated the reproduction of conservative social norms. In *The Female Eunuch* (1970) for instance, Germaine Greer famously argued that romance novels encouraged women to cherish 'the chains of their own bondage' (1971: 180). Indeed, as Joanne Hollows outlines in *Feminism, Femininity and Popular Culture* (2000) this critical outlook on romance fiction, seen also in the work of other second-wave critics such Kate Millett and Shulamith Firestone was all part of a more general resistance towards the idea of 'romance' within culture as a whole – it was seen as a means of reinforcing existing, societal structures and expectations and distracting women from the reality of their own exploitation and manipulation (72).

Romance fiction would begin to attract more sustained and nuanced analysis from the 1980s onwards, although some feminist critics still had major reservations. Tanya Modleski's *Loving with a Vengeance: Mass Produced Fantasies for Women* (1982) devoted a chapter to Harlequin Romances and concluded that whilst they did provide a valuable outlet for the expression of female dissatisfaction with male–female relationships, they also never questioned the primacy of these relationships, or of the patriarchal myths and institutions that underpin society. Janice A. Radway's *Reading the Romance* (1984) linked the meaning of the romance-reading experience to the need for emotional release desired by her sample group, who had otherwise subordinated their own desires to those of their families.

Many of the conclusions reached by Radway and Modleski would themselves be critiqued by another important study of the genre,

Pamela Regis's *A Natural History of the Romance Novel* (2003), in which it is argued that the genre has been sorely misunderstood by literary critics, in part because the second-wave feminists saw the romance novel, as she puts it, as 'an enslaver of women' that reinforced heterosexual and patriarchal ideology (6). Later discussions of romance fiction and its various offshoots – such as the Chick-Lit boom of the 1990s – would inspire a similarly diverse range of critical opinions, often coalescing around the question of whether or not the romance itself (and the act of reading the romance) can be seen as a liberating or ultimately anti-feminist act. More recently, we can also see these kinds of arguments revolve around post-2000 bestsellers such as the *Twilight* saga and *The Fifty Shades* series.

Feminist readings have by now been applied to every popular genre, with crime fiction and science fiction in particular having attracted much commentary of this nature, in part perhaps because both genres attracted explicitly feminist authors in the 1970s and after. Within crime fiction, female private detectives and police officers became increasingly significant (and of course, 'Golden Age' of the 1930s and 1940s detective fiction had some very notable women authors, most famously Agatha Christie and Dorothy Sayers). The built-in ability of both SF and fantasy to offer imaginative alternatives to the world as we currently understand it was particularly attractive to feminist authors such as Sherri S. Tepper, Octavia Butler, Joanna Russ, Alice Sheldon (better known as 'James Tiptree Jr.') and Ursula K. Le Guin during the 1970s and after. Although the two most influential feminist studies of the horror genre – *Men, Women and Chain Saws*: *Gender in the Modern Horror Film* (1992) by Carol J. Clover and *The Monstrous-Feminine*: *Film, Feminism and Psychoanalysis* (1993) by Barbara Creed – focus on film rather than fiction, they were hugely influential for critical considerations of the genre as a whole, particularly because they explored the way in which women were so often depicted as the monstrous 'Other' in horror narratives.

Because part of the feminist project is to unearth and celebrate the work of women writers and texts that have been neglected or forgotten about, texts from a wide range of genres and sub-genres are now being looked at from fresh perspectives, and further demonstrate popular fiction's capacity for telling stories about marginalised individuals even within mass culture itself. For instance, as Kaye Mitchell (2012) notes, there was a thriving market for lesbian pulp fiction in the US in the 1950s and 1960s, and, as she observes, whilst many of these books were written largely for the titillation of an assumed male reader, their frank representation of same-sex relationships meant that they assumed considerable cultural importance for women who otherwise felt completely unrepresented within mainstream heterosexual culture (130). Similarly, literary critics more generally are now paying much closer attention to popular fiction written by female writers in the eighteenth, nineteenth and early twentieth centuries.

The growing prominence of the feminist approach to literary studies has also helped focus greater attention on issues related to gender and sexuality in a more general sense. Since the 1990s in particular, critical work exploring representations of masculinity as well as characters and issues related to LGBTQ topics has become more visible. The field of 'Masculinity Studies' (or 'Men's Studies' as it is sometimes called) draws upon the work of sociologists such as Michael Kimmel and R. W. Connell and is particularly concerned with exploring what are said to be the often stifling and repressive hegemonic expectations of masculinity and the construction of masculine identity. As within feminism, exploring the way in which social and cultural expectations of gendered behaviour are created involves looking at the way in which certain representations manifest themselves within popular culture, including popular fiction.

In *Masculinity in Fiction and Film: Representing Men in Popular Genres, 1945–2000* (2006), Brian Baker discusses science fiction, fantasy and spy fiction in a bid to explore the relationship between representations of masculinity in popular genres and their link with the ideological imperatives of the American and British nation states during and after the Cold War era, arguing that these forms of masculinity reveal much about 'the cultural, social and political formations of their period of production' (vii). Other critics have discussed specific genres from this perspective, as is the case in Lee Clarke Mitchell's work on 'the persistent obsession with masculinity associated with the Western' (3), or Andrea Ochsner's 2011 discussion of the so-called 'Lad lit' sub-genre that emerged during the 1990s. However, as Ochsner also points out, there are still relatively few critical discussions on the topic of masculinity in popular fiction to date.

Another important and relatively recent development has been the emergence of theorists who examine popular fiction from an LGBTQ perspective as well as from a 'Queer Theory' perspective. This opening up to alternative viewpoints – and in particular, this exploration of issues explicitly related to complex and evolving questions of sexual orientation and gender identity – is itself arguably representative of the growing interest in and acceptance of diverse and at one time marginalised perspectives demonstrative of the postmodern turn in literary studies. There has been considerable work done on the representation of LGBTQ characters and themes within three popular genres in particular: horror and the gothic (whose foregrounding of the 'monstrous' other since the very beginnings of the genre has often lent itself to interpretations of this sort, as critics such as Paulina Palmer and George E. Haggerty have outlined), crime fiction and science fiction. As the editors of *Queer Universes: Sexualities in Science Fiction* (2008) note, 'If we take the central task of Queer Theory as the work of imagining a world in which all lives are liveable, we understand Queer Theory as being both utopian and Science Fictional, in the sense of imagining a future that opens out, rather than forecloses possibilities for becoming real, for mattering in the world' (5). As is the case within literary studies in general, the fact that critics are now willing to appraise popular texts from within a wide variety of theoretical and ideological perspectives related to the depiction of gender, sexuality and sexual orientation is yet another indication that popular fiction studies is becoming an ever more richly diverse and expansive field of academic inquiry.

Bibliography

Baker, Brian (2006), *Masculinity in Fiction and Film: Representing Men in Popular Genres, 1945–2000*, London: Continuum.

Carr, Helen (ed.) (1989), *From My Guy to Sci-Fi: Genre and Women's Writing in the Postmodern World*, London: Pandora.

Cranny-Francis, Anne (1990), *Feminist Fiction: Feminist Uses of Generic Fiction*, New York: St Martin's Press.

Gordon, Joan, Hollinger, Veronica and Pearson, Wendy Gay (eds) (2008), *Queer Universes: Sexualities in Science Fiction*, Liverpool: Liverpool University Press.

Greer, Germaine (1971), *The Female Eunuch*, London: Paladin.

Hollows, Joanne (2000), *Feminism, Femininity and Popular Culture*, Manchester and New York: Manchester University Press.

Kinsman, Margaret (2010), 'Feminist Crime Fiction', in C. Nickerson (ed.), *The Cambridge Companion to American Crime Fiction*, Cambridge: Cambridge University Press, pp. 148–63.

Makinen, Merja (2001), *Feminist Popular Fiction*, Basingstoke: Palgrave Macmillan.

Mitchell, Kaye (2012), 'Gender and Sexuality in Popular Fiction', in. D. Glover and S. McCracken (eds), *The Cambridge Companion to Popular Fiction*, Cambridge: Cambridge University Press, pp. 122–40.

Mitchell, Lee Clark (2006), *The Western: Making the Man in Fiction and Film*, Chicago: The University of Chicago Press.

Munford, Rebecca and Waters, Melanie (eds) (2014), *Feminism and Popular Culture: Investigating the Postfeminist Mystique*, New Brunswick, NJ: Rutgers University Press.

Ochsner, Andrea (2011), 'Who is that Man? Lad Trouble in *High Fidelity*, *The Best a Man Can Get* and *White City Blue*, in S. Horlacher (ed.), *Constructions of Masculinity in British Literature from the Middle Ages to the Present*, Basingstoke: Palgrave Macmillan, pp. 247–67.

Radford, Jean (ed.) (1986), *The Progress of Romance: The Politics of Popular Fiction*, London: Routledge and Kegan Paul.

Radway, Janice A. (1984), *Reading the Romance*, Chapael Hill: North Carolina University Press.

Regis, Pamela (2003), *A Natural History of the Romance Novel*, Philadelphia: University of Pennsylvania Press.

Rich, Jennifer (2007), *An Introduction to Modern Feminist Theory*, Tirril: Humanities-EBooks.

Russ, Joanna (1995), *'To Write Like a Woman': Essays on Feminism and Science Fiction*, Bloomington: Indiana University Press.

Whelehan, Imelda (2005), *The Feminist Bestseller: From Sex and the Single Girl to Sex and the City*, Basingstoke: Palgrave Macmillan.

Wolmarck, Jenny (1986), *Aliens and Others: Science Fiction, Feminism and Postmodernism*, Iowa City: University of Iowa Press.

9. Ecocriticism and Popular Fiction

Within a North American context in particular, the ecocritical approach to literature has proved to be one of the major critical approaches to have emerged in recent decades, and as such, it is hardly surprising that it has also gradually begun to influence popular fiction studies. Ecocriticism, which began in US and UK universities in the early 1980s, focuses, as Cheryll Glotfelty has put it, 'on the relationship between literature and the natural environment' (1996: xviii). It is an area of critical inquiry that has taken on particular significance in recent years due to the ever-accelerating sense of environmental crisis informed by the fact that, as all but the most ideologically-blinkered observers would acknowledge, the effects of global climate change are becoming devastatingly apparent.

One of the most obvious manifestations of ecological anxiety within popular fiction has been the emergence of the (purportedly) new science fiction sub-genre known as 'Cli-Fi' (or 'Climate Change Fiction'), although, as several well-known science fiction authors have rightly pointed out, the genre has been dramatising ecological anxieties related to global warming for decades (J. G. Ballard's novel *The Drowned World* depicted a future London ravaged by the consequences of solar radiation as far back as 1962). Because the horror and science fiction genres in particular lend themselves so well to the depiction of worst-case scenarios, and because dystopian science fiction in particular so often draws upon political and social undercurrents within the culture of that particular moment, the most significant pop-fiction related to eco-critical interventions have to date focused upon these two genres.

The publication in 2012 of the essay collection *Ecogothic* (edited by Andrew Smith and William Hughes) represented the first major study of how the gothic genre engages with images of environmental catastrophe, the wilderness, nature and the post-eco apocalypse world, and it has since become a significant area of emerging interest within horror and gothic studies. The term 'eco-horror' is also used within this context to describe the many 'Revenge of Nature' narratives that have manifested themselves since the 1970s in particular. The eco-critical approach has also been persuasively applied to science fiction texts and authors (as in Frederick Buell's *From Apocalypse to Way of Life*, 2004), which contains an excellent chapter on depictions of environmental crisis in popular literature and film), as well as books such as *Green Planets: Ecology and Science Fiction* (2014). A wider range of popular genres, including crime, are discussed by Patrick Murphy in his book *Ecocritical Explorations in Literary and Cultural Studies: Fences, Boundaries and Fields* (2010), which also discusses the way in which popular fiction has engaged with issues of ecological significance. Environmental anxieties have frequently manifested themselves within YA fiction in recent years, with series such as *The Carbon Diaries: 2015* (2009) by Saci Lloyd, *Blood Red Road* by Moira Young (2011), *Breathe* by Sarah Crossan (2012) and *The Ship* by Antonia Honeywell (2015), all of which feature a world devastated by global warning and its ecological and political consequences.

Bibliography

Buell, Frederick (2004), *From Apocalypse to Way of Life: Environmental Crisis in the American Century*, New York: Routledge.

Garrard, Greg (2004), *Ecocriticism*, London: Routledge.

Glotfelty, Cheryll (1996), 'Introduction', in C. Glotfelty and H. Fromm (eds),

The Ecocriticism Reader: Landmarks in Literary Ecology, Athens: The University of Georgia Press, pp. xv–xxxvii

Hughes, William and Andrew Smith (eds) (2013), *Ecogothic*, Manchester: Manchester University Press.

Murphy, Patrick (2010), *Ecocritical Explorations in Literary and Cultural Studies: Fences, Boundaries and Fields,* Lanham, MD: Lexington.

Tonn, Shara (2015), 'Cli-Fi – That's Climate Fiction – is the new Sci-Fi', Wired, 17 July, <http://www.wired.com/2015/07/cli-fi-thats-climate-fiction-new-sci-fi/> (last accessed 15 April 2015).

Ullrich, J. K. (2015), 'Climate Fiction: Can Books Save the Planet?', *The Atlantic*, 14 August, <http://www.theatlantic.com/entertainment/archive/2015/08/climate-fiction-margaret-atwood-literature/400112/>(last accessed 15 April 2016).

Major Popular Genres

Fantasy

There have been many attempts to define fantasy, but one of the most useful recent definitions is that provided by Farah Mendlesohn and Edward James, which also persuasively distinguishes it from the genre it is most often conflated with: 'The most obvious construction of fantasy in literature and art is the presence of the impossible and the unexplainable. This tends to cut out most science fiction, which, while it may deal with the impossible, regards everything as [rationally] explicable' (2009: 3). In *Fantasy: The Literature of Subversion* (1981), Rosemary Jackson notes that the term 'fantasy' has traditionally been applied rather indiscriminately to any form of literature that does not give priority to realistic representation.

'Commercial' or 'genre' fantasy in its current incarnation owes an immense debt to the work of J. R. R. Tolkien, in that without the phenomenal success of *The Lord of the Rings* series (1954–5) the genre's landscape would likely be very different today. Brian Attebery even suggests that Tolkien is largely responsible for 'separating fantasy from its ancestral forms' (1992: XIII). Indeed, many of the most notable tropes present in the modern 'epic' fantasy novel are strongly influenced by his legacy. However, it is important to note that there are also clear pop fiction antecedents of this variety of fantasy that predate Tolkien, such as the American pulp magazines of the 1920s and 1930s that did much to establish the 'Sword and Sorcery' tradition. In addition, it should also be stressed that fantasy also has a large number of sub-genres, recurrent tropes and thematic concerns which differ substantially from the 'secondary world' heroic fantasy type, as the exhaustive reference work *The Encyclopaedia of Fantasy* (freely available online) demonstrates.

Since 2000, fantasy children's literature has made a major contribution to the current commercial prominence of the genre. As Clive Bloom notes, the work of Philip Pullman and J. K. Rowling is pivotal in this regard (2008: 275). The genre has also benefited from the success of high-profile film and television adaptations of classic novels, such as Peter Jackson's blockbuster *The Lord of the Rings* trilogy (2001–3) and the critically acclaimed television series *Game of Thrones* (2011–), which adapts George R. R. Martin's *A Song of Ice and Fire* series (1996–). Martin's bleak worldview and uncompromising sex and violence also helped establish the 'Grimdark' sub-genre, which has been characterised as a reaction to the supposedly 'sanitised' epic fantasy of the past.

Another major fantasy trend of recent years has been the emergence of 'Urban Fantasy'. Urban Fantasy in its current incarnation features savvy, street-smart protagonists (often investigators of some sort) who live in contemporary cityscapes in which the fantastical and the supernatural exist alongside everyday reality. It has proved particularly popular with female readers and authors (although there are also many prominent male authors and protagonists). Though Urban Fantasy is a relatively new publishing category, like fantasy in the broadest sense of the term, it still revolves around the relationship between 'the magical, the strange, the weird, the wondrous', and 'the mundane, the world we know' (Guran 2011: 145).

Bibliography

Attebury, Brian (1992), *Strategies of Fantasy*, Bloomington: Indiana University Press.

Bloom, Clive (2008), *Bestsellers: Popular Fiction since 1900*, Basingstoke: Palgrave Macmillan.

Clute, John and John Grant (eds), *The Encyclopaedia of Fantasy* <http://sf-en cyclopedia.uk/fe.php/>.

Guran, P. (2011), 'A Funny Thing Happened on the Way to Urban Fantasy', in P. S. Beagle and J. R. Lansdale (eds), *The Urban Fantasy Anthology*, San Francisco: Tachyon Publications, pp. 137–45.

Hume, Kathryn (2014), *Fantasy and Mimesis: Responses to Reality in Western Literature*, London: Routledge.

Jackson, Rosemary (1981), *Fantasy: The Literature of Subversion*, London: Methuen & Co. Ltd.

James, Edward and Farah Mendlesohn (2009), *A Short History of Fantasy*, London: Middlesex University Press.

James, Edward and Farah Mendlesohn (2012), *The Cambridge Companion to Fantasy Literature*, Cambridge: Cambridge University Press.

Stableford, Brian (2009), *The A–Z of Fantasy Literature*, Lanham: Scarecrow Press.

Horror

Horror is, revealingly, the only genre with a name that derives from an emotional response. Although other genres may of course include occasional moments of 'horror', one may reasonably say that within the horror genre, the evocation of dread, disgust and *fear* is the prime intention of the author. Of course, the variety of fear being elicited may differ widely depending on what one is reading, and one's own emotional and psychological trigger points.

The terms 'horror' and 'gothic' are often used interchangeably by critics and readers, and, as Clive Bloom has usefully observed, there exists 'a multiplicity of apparently substitutable terms to cover the same thing – gothic tale, ghost tale, terror romance, gothic horror . . . it becomes clear that while "horror" and "gothic" are often (if not usually) interchangeable, there are, of course, gothic tales that are not horror fiction (Daphne du Maurier's *Rebecca* is a good example) and horror tales that contain no real gothic elements (Elizabeth Bowen's "The Cat Jumps")' (2000: 155). The horror genre is, however, an offshoot of the wider gothic tradition, and many of the genre's most distinctive settings and patterns had their beginnings there. In addition, horror narratives almost always have a threatening 'Other' although that 'Other' can be of both internal and external origin.

Horror fiction can be divided into two basic categories: supernatural and non-supernatural. In the supernatural horror tale, unease is usually created by the violation of the supposedly orderly, rational laws of nature. Supernatural horror fiction often features monsters that in equal measure attract and repulse. They frequently dramatise aspects of ourselves that we find objectionable but inescapable.

The non-supernatural horror tale has become increasingly significant since the end of the Second World War, when the real-life horrors of the Holocaust and the advent of the nuclear age prompted a move away from more fantastical terrors to horror narratives set in everyday locales that dramatise fears arising from human rather than external monstrosity. Many of the genre's most effective post-1950s narratives are related from the perspective of characters unable to reliably differentiate between reality and fantasy. Mental instability and outright psychopathy often feature. This is why it is the figure of the serial killer that represents modern horror fiction's most emblematic modern 'Other' (serial killers regularly feature in crime novels and thrillers as well, meaning that the lines between the genres are often blurred these days).

One of the most notable post-2000 trends within horror fiction has been the popularity of apocalyptic narratives, especially those featuring zombies (although vampires, climate change and killer viruses have all featured too). Although horror fiction is no longer the high-profile commercial publishing category it was during the 1970s and 1980s, one of the best-selling authors of the past forty years, Stephen King, is best known for horror fiction (although he has written in other genres, most notably crime, of late). The small-press horror scene is also thriving and, as the 'Creepypasta' phenomenon indicates, horror fiction has found a receptive new home online. Many supernatural horror tropes have also recently been assimilated into the paranormal romance and urban fantasy sub-genres, both of which frequently feature werewolves, ghosts, witches, demons and vampires.

Bibliography

Bloom, Clive (2000), 'Horror Fiction: In Search of a Definition', in D. Punter (ed.), *A Companion to the Gothic*, Oxford: Wiley Blackwell, pp. 155–66.

Carroll, Noel (1990), *The Philosophy of Horror: Or, Paradoxes of the Heart*, New York: Routledge.

Lovecraft, H. P. [1927] (2012), 'Supernatural Horror in Literature', in S. T. Joshi (ed.), *The Annotated Supernatural Horror in Literature*, New York: Hippocampus Press [online].

Nelson, Victoria (2012), *Gothika: Vampire Heroes, Human Gods, and the New Supernatural*, Cambridge, MA: Harvard University Press.

Reyes, Xavier Aldana (ed.) (2016), *Horror: A Literary History*, London: British Library.

Skal, David J. (1994), *The Monster Show: A Cultural History of Horror*, London: Plexus.

Wisker, Gina (2005), *Horror Fiction: An Introduction*, New York: Continuum.

Science Fiction

Science fiction is often said to be the most intellectually and philosophically ambitious variety of popular fiction. It grapples with many of the most urgent questions associated with life as a rational, questioning human being; indeed, problematising just what it means to be human has long been one of the genre's main narrative tropes. Another key preoccupation is the genre's interest in the transformative potential of scientific and technological advances. George Slusser contends that 'Science Fiction is about science. It is the sole literary form that examines the ways in which science penetrates, alters, and transforms the themes, forms and world view of fiction' (2008: 27).

As Peter Nicholls notes, in the *Encyclopaedia of Science Fiction*, the term 'science fiction' did not become widely used until the 1950s, although genre science fiction was already becoming recognisable as a distinct literary category by that stage (1999: 569). However, though it did not become named or defined until the late nineteenth and early twentieth centuries, many of the elements, story templates and preoccupations we now associate with SF were formulated centuries before. The generally accepted origins of modern science fiction are said to have begun in the Renaissance, and most particularly in the utopian writings of authors such as Thomas More, Frances Bacon and Jonathan Swift (Pringle 1997: 8–18). Mary Shelley's *Frankenstein* (1818) provided the genre with what would become one of its most familiar storylines: that of the arrogant scientist who allows the thrill of invention to blind him to the terrible consequences of his actions.

By the mid-nineteenth century a number of prominent American writers had what we would now consider proto-SF elements in their work (Nicholls 1999: 568). However, the author who perhaps made the greatest impact upon the nineteenth-century popular imagination was Jules Verne, whose second novel, *Journey to the Centre of the Earth* (1864), is considered the first great 'scientific romance'. In the 1890s, the novels of H. G. Wells helped mark the beginnings of modern science fiction (Booker and Thomas 2009: 6). The American pulp magazines of the late nineteenth and early twentieth centuries also played a crucial role in establishing and shaping the genre as a recognisable publishing category (Ashley 2008: 61). In 1926, the publication of the inaugural issue of the magazine *Amazing Stories* saw the first ever English-language magazine dedicated to science fiction stories.

The success of *Amazing Stories* inspired the launch of a host of rival publications, foremost amongst them *Astounding Science Fiction* (1930). Editor John Campbell helped usher in the so-called 'Golden Age' of American science fiction. Although the 'Golden Age' was dominated by American authors, the process of maturation it underwent during the 1960s and 1970s owed much to the work of British writers such as Michael Moorcock, J. G. Ballard and Brian W. Aldiss. In the 1970s and after, female authors such as Ursula K. Le Guin, Joanna Russ, Sheri S. Tepper, Kate Wilhelm and Margaret

Atwood used the genre as a means to dramatise issues relating to the way in which women are treated in society. Richly imaginative explorations of issues of race and sexuality also became increasingly common. As the so-called 'Sad Puppies' controversy surrounding the 2015 Hugo Awards has indicated, however, not every genre enthusiast has welcomed the increasingly 'progressive' nature of the genre.

Since the mid-twentieth century, science fiction has become an evermore intellectually ambitious and thematically rich genre. Although utopian visions, like the planetary romances and the 'psychic powers' tales of the 1950s have largely fallen out of favour, the dystopian narrative, tellingly, has come roaring back into fashion since the mid-2000s, and remains the sub-genre most likely to be tackled by 'literary' authors. The academic study of science fiction is thriving, with present-day critics building on the work of earlier academics such as Darko Suvin, whose concept of the 'Novuum' – the kind of 'strange newness' that creates the 'cognitive estrangement' he identifies as being a basic building block of the genre – has become a core critical concept. However, in recent years, science fiction has been eclipsed in popularity by fantasy, probably because fantasy is considered by many readers to be a more 'accessible' form of imaginative fiction. Sales figures released by *Publisher's Weekly* related to the 'Hottest (and Coldest) Book Categories of 2014' suggested that sales of adult SF had also been hit hard by the success of YA titles belonging to the 'Science Fiction/Fantasy/Magic' categories.

Bibliography

Ashley, M. (2008), 'Science Fiction Magazines: The Crucibles of Change', in D. Seed (ed.), *A Companion to Science Fiction*, Oxford: Blackwell, pp. 60–76.

Booker, M. Keith and Anne-Marie Thomas (eds) (2009), *The Science Fiction Handbook*, Chichester: Wiley Blackwell.

Clute, John and Peter Nicholls (eds) (1999), *The Encyclopaedia of Science Fiction*, London: Orbit.

Landon, Brooks (2002), *Science Fiction after 1900: From the Steam Man to the Stars*, London: Routledge.

Pringle, David (1997), *The Ultimate Encyclopaedia of Science Fiction: The Definitive Illustrated Guide*, London: Carlton.

Roberts, Adam (2000), *Science Fiction*, London: Routledge.

Slusser, George (2008), 'The Origins of Science Fiction', in D. Seed (ed.), *A Companion to Science Fiction*, Oxford: Blackwell, pp. 27–42.

Suvin, Darko (1979), *Metamorphoses of Science Fiction*, New Haven, CT: Yale University Press.

Crime

Crime has for decades been one of the most commercially successful forms of popular fiction. The problem that faces us when we attempt to neatly define crime fiction is a familiar one when it comes to discussing popular genres: the term encompasses multiple sub-genres and narrative strategies. In the broadest sense, however, crime fiction narratives tend to conform to much the same basic structure: a crime is committed (often, but not by any means *always*, a murder); the crime is investigated, either by a professional detective or an amateur sleuth; and some kind of resolution or form of justice is achieved in the closing stages of the text. However, many novels clustered under the 'crime fiction' heading by publishers, booksellers and readers bypass, subvert, or ignore these conventions.

Literary antecedents to the crime novel can be found hundreds, even thousands of years ago. As Barry Forshaw notes, criminal acts – and in particular, murder – provide the plot engines for many of the most famous works of literature ever written (2007: 1). Stephen Knight points out that so-called 'murder pamphlets' containing the lurid details of grisly true crimes were very popular during Elizabethan and Jacobean times, whilst Harold Schecter has shown that from the earliest days of European settlement, North American readers were also fascinated by accounts of real-life criminal atrocities (2008). One of the most important proto-crime novels was William Godwin's *Caleb Williams* (1794), the tale of a moral young man who is wrongly accused of murder. In American literature at about the same time, there appeared Charles Brockden Brown's *Edgar Huntly* (1799), which has been described as 'America's first detective novel'. Another American, the ever-adaptable Edgar Allan Poe, is an even more key figure, due to his creation of the French detective C. Auguste Dupin, a major influence upon Arthur Conan Doyle's Sherlock Holmes. Dupin's process of deductive reasoning helped establish the 'puzzle' aspect of the genre as one of its key attractions.

In the mid to late nineteenth century, novels grouped together under the banner of so-called 'Sensation Fiction' often included strong elements of the crime novel. This was perhaps most notable in the work of Wilkie Collins, whose 1868 novel *The Moonstone* helped popularise the figure of the professional detective (Knight 2010: 44). The police procedural and its various off-shoots (such as the tale of forensic detection) remains one of the major sub-genres of crime fiction to this day.

In the early to mid-twentieth century, there emerged a number of authors whose contributions to detective fiction consolidated the commercial popularity of the genre. By far the most celebrated author was Agatha Christie. P. D. James – herself a towering figure within the genre – has suggested that Christie's appeal lies in what readers perceive to be her evocation of a romanticised, rural England in which society consists of a neatly ordered hierarchy in which everyone knows their place (2011: 97). However, Christie's work also had a genuine ruthlessness to it that complicates perceptions of her as an inherently 'reassuring' author.

As Lee Horsley notes, the crime writing tradition became steadily more diverse throughout the twentieth century (2010: 28). In the United States, the archetype of the cynical, hard-bitten private investigator became the basis for seminal novels by writers such as Raymond Chandler, Dashiell Hammett and Micky Spillane. A new degree of psychological complexity and realism had begun to emerge in the late 1940s and after, particularly in the work of authors such as Dorothy B. Hughes, Jim Thompson, Patricia Highsmith and Ruth Rendell. Crime fiction also increasingly featured protagonists and plotlines that represented previously marginalised sectors of society.

One of the major post-2000 trends in crime fiction is the 'Nordic Noir' phenomenon, which refers to the boom in crime writing from Scandinavia, influenced by the huge sales that accompanied the publication in English translation of Swedish author Stieg Larsson's *Millennium* trilogy. The trend helped make English-language publishers (and readers) much more receptive to translated fiction from 'international' authors, many of whom had long been bestsellers in their home countries.

Bibliography

Edwards, Martin (2015), *The Golden Age of Murder: The Mystery of the Writers who Invented the Modern Detective Story*, London: Harper Collins.
Forshaw, Barry (2007), *The Rough Guide to Crime Fiction*, London: Rough Guides.
Horsley, Lee (2005), *Twentieth-Century Crime Fiction*, Oxford: Oxford University Press.

Horsley, Lee (2010), 'From Sherlock Holmes to the Present', in Lee Horsley and C. J. Rzepka (eds), *A Companion to Crime Fiction*, Oxford: Wiley Blackwell, pp. 28–42.

James, P. D. (2011), *Talking about Detective Fiction*, New York: Vintage.

Knight, Stephen (2010), *Crime Fiction since 1800: Detection, Death, Diversity*, Basingstoke: Palgrave Macmillan.

Priestman, Martin (ed.) (2003), *The Cambridge Companion to Crime Fiction*, Cambridge: Cambridge University Press.

Schecter, Harold (ed.) (2008), *True Crime: An American Anthology*, New York: Library of America.

Romance

In its original usage the term 'romance' was (and still is) deployed in relation to medieval and Renaissance works of fiction featuring an emphasis on martial deeds as well as scenes of courtship and love. It has also been used to describe the work of authors writing in a non-realist or allegorical vein. Within a popular fiction context, however, the term always refers to stories in which the main focus of narrative interest development is a romantic relationship. As Pamela Regis argues, 'A romance novel is a work of prose fiction that tells the story of the courtship and betrothal of one or more heroines' (2003: 22). However, as Regis and others have noted, marriage is by no means always the outcome in contemporary romance novels, which increasingly reflect the financial and social independence of their overwhelmingly female readers. Statistics on the Romance Writers of America (RWA) website indicate, at the time of writing, that 84 per cent of American romance novel writers are female.

A romance may be set in any time period ('historicals' have always been very popular). It may have a heroine and hero of any socio-economic, religious, national or educational background. Increasingly, the genre has become more diverse, and it is now not uncommon to find non-white characters as well as gay, lesbian and bisexual protagonists and love interests. Romance novels also differ widely in terms of how sexually explicit they are: whilst some are relatively chaste, other titles are quite explicit; indeed, every major romance publisher now has a dedicated erotica line. Although many publishers issue specific guidelines as to what they are looking for in relation to a specific imprint, the scope of the genre in general is therefore quite broad. However, it has been argued that no matter what form they take, romance novels will always contain certain recurrent characteristics.

Indeed, Regis's contention that romance novels must always include 'eight essential elements' is one of the genre's key critical assertions:

> In one or more scenes, romance novels always depict the following: the initial state of the society in which the hero and heroine must court, the meeting between hero and heroine, the barrier to the union of hero and heroine, the attraction between heroine and hero, the declaration of love between heroine and hero, the point of ritual death, the recognition by heroine and hero of the means to overcome the barrier, and the betrothal. These elements are essential. (2003: 30)

Romance fiction has traditionally been one of the most academically neglected categories of popular fiction. Writing in 1982, Tania Modleski critiqued the 'double-critical standard' that meant that the then largely male body of 'mass culture' critics had either ignored or overlooked 'popular feminine narratives', and argued that this was because of a bias within Western culture towards male heroes and male texts (1982: 12–13). Writing more recently, however, Regis attributes much of the critical neglect of the genre to what she sees as the tendency amongst feminist critics of the 1970s and 1980s to unfairly characterise the romance as a form of fiction that denies the heroine an independent and fully individuated life outside of traditional models of love and marriage (2003: 13).

Critical debate surrounding the genre still is inclined to focus on exploring whether or not romance fiction tends to reinforce conventional gender roles and expectations (by making love, courtship and, traditionally, marriage, the central interest of the heroine's life) or to subvert them, by dramatising themes surrounding intimate relationships and providing a cathartic escape from everyday life. During the 1990s, the Chick-Lit sub-genre – which featured urban-based heroines who self-effacingly juggled demanding careers with the quest for love – aroused controversy amongst feminist commentators who variously saw novels such as *Bridget Jones's Diary* as either an endorsement of or betrayal of the benefits reaped by second-wave feminism.

Eighteenth- and nineteenth-century antecedents to the genre are fairly easy to identify. These include *Pamela* (1740) by Samuel Richardson, *Pride and Prejudice* (1813) by Jane Austen and *Jane Eyre* (1847) by Charlotte Bronte. It took rather longer, however, for the commercial romance novel as we would recognise it today to emerge. A burst of popularity for the so-called 'gothic romance' during the late 1960s and early 1970s helped create the commercial conditions in which authors such as Rosemary Rogers, Kathleen Woodwiss, Janet Dailey and Jayne Ann Krentz came to prominence during the late 1970s and after. Regis also identifies the British writers Georgette Heyer (queen of the 'Regency Romance') and romantic suspense author Mary Stewart as being key figures in establishing the romance as a major publishing category. By far the most high-profile romance author of the past two decades is Nora Roberts, who has, to date, published more than 200 novels.

Romance fiction in what is known as the 'category' market owes much to the British publishing firm Mills & Boon, and Canadian publisher Harlequin, which for many decades has been the most prolific producer of 'category' romance fiction in the world (Harlequin has owned Mills & Boon since 1971). As Maryan Wherry notes, 'category' romances 'are published under a common imprint or series name, released at standard intervals, and frequently identified by sequential numbers of a particular line' (2014: 57). Harlequin currently publishes up to eighty-five novels a month.

Since 2000, the 'paranormal romance' has become one of the most notable newer sub-genres, thanks in part to the immense popular and commercial success of the *Twilight* trilogy (2005–8). In recent years, the advent of e-books and e-readers has meant that the romance has benefited from having an even more streamlined and accessible delivery system. E. L. James's *Fifty Shades of Grey* (2011) was a particularly high-profile beneficiary of the ease and anonymity of the digital download. Digital-only romance publishers and imprints have become increasingly common, and according to the RWA website, around 40 per cent of romance novels in the US are now sold digitally.

Bibliography

Harzewski, Stephanie (2011), *Chick Lit and Postfeminism*, Charlottesville: University of Virginia Press.

McCracken, Scott (1998), 'Popular Romance', in *Pulp: Reading Popular Fiction*, Manchester: Manchester University Press, pp. 75–101.

Modleski, Tanya (1982), *Loving With a Vengeance: Mass-Produced Fantasies for Women*, Hamden: Archon.

Radway, Janice A. (1984), *Reading the Romance*, Chapel Hill: University of North Carolina Press.

Regis, Pamela (2003), *A Natural History of the Romance Novel*, Philadelphia: University of Pennsylvania Press.

Wherry, Maryan (2014), 'More than a Love Story: The Complexities of the Popular Romance', in C. Berberich (ed.), *The Bloomsbury Introduction to Popular Fiction*, London: Bloomsbury, pp. 53–69.

Thriller

As Martin Rubin acknowledges in his Introduction to a book on films that belong to this generic category, 'the label *thriller* is widely used but highly problematic' (1999: 3). In short, it is problematic because 'thriller' is in fact a very broad descriptive term: the 'concept of "thriller" falls somewhere between a genre proper and a descriptive quality that is attached to other, more clearly defined genres, such as spy thriller, detective thriller, horror thriller' (Rubin 1999: 3). What the term 'thriller' *does* suggest is a narrative in which the main protagonist is in peril from quite early on. Indeed, as Philip Simpson notes '"thriller" in the generic sense, tends to connote an emphasis on physical danger and action over in-depth character study', a tendency that owes much to its origins in late nineteenth-century pulp and sensation fiction (2010: 187). A thriller, then, need not begin (or even end) with a mystery that must be solved, but regardless of the specifics, the protagonist often faces considerable danger quite early on, and usually a powerful antagonist of some sort, be it a specific person (a dangerous criminal, a corrupt politician, a rogue scientist, their own spouse) or a system (a secret organisation, a government, a dangerous group). Escalating anxiety is therefore a major characteristic. David Glover notes, 'the thriller was and still is to a large extent marked by the way in which it persistently seeks to raise the stakes of the narrative, heightening or exaggerating the experience of events by transforming them into a rising curve of danger, violence or shock' (2003: 138). Sub-categories include the psychological thriller, or 'psycho thriller' (in which the state of mind of the protagonist or antagonist is of paramount narrative significance), as well as thrillers related to specific professions, scenarios or threats – these include legal thrillers, medical thrillers, techno thrillers, spy thrillers, serial killer thrillers, political thrillers and supernatural thrillers. Although, as Glover says, many thrillers do feature an investigative or deductive element (such as the ingenious variation on the 'locked-room' murder mystery that represents one of the major plot strands in Stieg Larsson's *The Girl with the Dragon Tattoo*), these features 'when present [. . .] necessarily occupy only a secondary role', thus distinguishing them from the detective story (2003: 137).

In recent years, many of the most high-profile thrillers on both sides of the Atlantic have belonged to the so-called 'Domestic Noir' sub-genre (the term was previously applied to certain female-focused noir films of the 1940s and 1950s), in which suspense and narrative action are generated by tensions and traumas arising from intimate relationships (be they marital or familial). These novels make frequent use of an unreliable narrator, as seen in the work of authors such as Gillian Flynn (whose 2012 novel *Gone Girl* was a masterpiece of narrative misdirection), S. J. Watson, Megan Abbott and Paula Hawkins. Hawkins's 2015 bestseller *The Girl on the Train* was a worldwide hit that rapidly outsold even *The Da Vinci Code* in hardback sales and spent sixteen consecutive weeks at the top of the NYT fiction bestseller list. Along with the rather condescending descriptor 'Chick Noir', the term 'Grip Lit' has also recently been used to describe these kinds of thrillers: it was first coined by the novelist Marian Keyes, who used it to explain her fondness for 'really gripping books' about 'very recognisable women who live messy lives'. At the time of writing, the 'Domestic Noir' boom shows no signs of fizzling out. The thriller has for many years been one of the most commercially successful varieties of popular fiction, perhaps in part because the successful thriller, by dint of the very nature of the genre, has to have a compelling 'hook', 'an intriguing element of originality, which draws the reader in', even if 'Some, even most of the rest of the material can be generic filler, over which the reader can skip or skim' (McCracken 2012: 112).

Bibliography

Glover, David (2003), 'The Thriller', in M. Priestman (ed.), *The Cambridge Companion to Crime Fiction*, Cambridge: Cambridge University Press, pp. 135–54.

Horsley, Lee (2001), *The Noir Thriller*, Basingstoke: Palgrave Macmillan.

Horsley, Lee (2005), 'Transgression and Pathology', in *Twentieth-Century Crime Fiction*, Oxford: Oxford University Press, pp. 112–57.

McCracken, Scott (2012), 'Reading Time: Popular Fiction and the Everyday', in D. Glover and S. McCracken (eds), *The Cambridge Companion to Popular Fiction*, Cambridge: Cambridge University Press, pp. 103–21.

Palmer, Jerry (1979), *Thrillers: Genesis and Structure of a Popular Genre*, London: St Martin's Press.

Rubin, Martin (1999), *Thrillers*, Cambridge: Cambridge University Press.

Simpson, Philip (2010), 'Noir and the Psycho Thriller', in C. J. Rzepka and

L. Horsley (eds), *A Companion to Crime Fiction*, Oxford: Wiley Blackwell, pp. 187–97.
Todorov, Tzvetan (1977), 'The Typology of Detective Fiction', in *The Poetics of Prose*, New York: Cornell University Press, pp. 42–51.

Comic Books and Graphic Novels

Comic books cannot be considered a genre in the way that the previous entries in this section can. Rather, they constitute a mode, and as such, individual titles can potentially encompass every conceivable popular genre. The most influential definition of the comic book is that provided by Scott McCloud in *Understanding Comics: The Invisible Art* (1993). Focusing on formal characteristics, McCloud argues that the comic consists of 'Juxtaposed pictorial and other images in a deliberate sequence intended to convey information and/or produce an aesthetic response in the reader' (9). This contention has, however, been challenged. Robert C. Harvey points out that McCloud's definition contends that comics do not have to contain words and counters by arguing that an essential criterion of the comic should be verbal content (2009: 25). It is therefore perhaps more useful to adopt the approach taken by researchers for whom 'part of the definition of comics relates to production and market as well besides a series of formal characteristics. According to such a definition, comics were "born" with the mass production of American newspaper comic strips in 1896' (Christiansen and Magnusson 2000: 10). Certainly, the three-panel newspaper strips that emerged at the end of the nineteenth century did a huge amount, as Roger Sabin (2001) has demonstrated, to help establish the mainstream comics industry. When enterprising publisher Max Gaines realised that cheap, affordable, stand-alone digests of popular newspaper strips would sell in big numbers, the 'comic book' was born.

In 1938, the arrival of Superman in the pages of *Action* comics (Batman would follow just a year later) marked the beginning of a major boom for the US comics industry. As Paul Gravett suggests, during the 1940s the black-and-white moral universes occupied by the nation's superheroes 'filled the modern pantheon that could answer an anxious public's longing for secular saviours to fight for them against crime and injustice on the streets and against the Nazis in the looming war in Europe' (2005: 75). However, whilst superhero titles were, then as now, extremely popular with readers, until the late

1950s US comics spanned a wide range of genres. Amongst the most popular were romance, western and war titles. Crime and horror titles were particularly popular until the introduction of the self-censoring 'Comics Code Authority' in 1954.

The United Kingdom also had its own vibrant (albeit much smaller) comics industry in the post-war era, when the likes of *Eagle* was established in part to counter the perceived immorality of imported American comics. As Gravett notes, in France and Japan 'Bandes dessinées' and 'Manga' had long achieved a level of critical respectability that it would take British and American comics decades to achieve. Well into the 1980s, the format was widely considered to be an inherently juvenile one in the US and UK, a perception fuelled by the fact that by far the most high-profile comics titles were superhero ones.

Marvel had a particularly stellar period in the 1960s, during which many of the company's most famous superheroes were created by their 'bullpen' of writers and artists (the most famous of whom included writer Stan Lee and artist Jack Kirby). However, by the late 1960s there also existed a thriving adult-orientated comics counterculture. In the UK, many of the most significant comics creators of the 1980s and 1990s – including Alan Moore, Brian Bolland, Neil Gaiman and Grant Morrison – got their big break working for the unabashedly violent and satirical science fiction comic *2000AD*. The so-called 'British invasion' of the US comics scene in the late 1980s dramatically changed the industry, and imprints such as DC's 'Vertigo' line began to target the more 'mature' reader. During the mid-1980s, revisionist superhero epics such as Alan Moore and Dave Gibbon's *Watchmen* (1986) and Frank Miller's *Batman: The Dark Knight Returns* (1986) helped reconfigure reader and critical expectations of the medium. At around the same time, the critical acclaim afforded the likes of Art Spiegelman's Holocaust memoir *Maus* (1980–91) helped establish the 'graphic novel' as a distinct commercial category.

Up until the early to mid-1980s, the descriptor 'graphic novel' was not widely used, even though publisher Richard Kyle coined the term in 1964 (Gravett 2005: 8). What that term actually means, and how the 'graphic novel' is supposedly different from the 'comic book' is still a matter of intense debate. Generally speaking, it is usually suggested that the 'graphic novel' represents a more ambitious, sophisticated and unified narrative than the supposedly more 'juvenile' comic book, although some writers and artists feel that this definition is more indicative of 'highbrow' snobbery towards comics readers and creators. Whether or not one believes that there is an inherent differ-ence between the 'comic book' and the 'graphic novel', however, it cannot be denied that increased critical respect for the medium has helped create a climate where writers and artists can explore a wide range of generic and thematic interests in their work. Although super-hero titles still dominate the market, since 2000 there have also been high-profile science fiction, horror, noir and fantasy comic releases, as well as acclaimed works of memoir and political reportage. As with every other kind of popular fiction, the advent of digital publishing been a game changer for the industry: comics can now be instantly downloaded at any time using apps such as Comixology, a develop-ment that appears to be attracting more female readers in particular.

Bibliography

Christiansen, Hans-Christian and Anne Magnusson (eds) (2000), *Comics and Culture: Analytical and Theoretical Approaches to Comics*, Copenhagen: Museum Tusculanum Press.

Gravett, Paul (2005), *Graphic Novels: Stories to Change Your Life*, London: Aurum Press.

Harvey, Robert C. (2009), 'How Comics Came to Be', in J. Heer and K. Worcester (eds), *A Comic Studies Reader*, Jackson: University Press of Mississippi, pp. 25–45.

Jones, Gerard (2004), *Men of Tomorrow: Geeks, Gangsters and the Birth of the Comic Book*, London: Random House.

McCloud, Scott (1993), *Understanding Comics: The Invisible Art*, New York: HarperCollins.

Morrison, Grant (2012), *Supergods: Our World in the Age of the Superhero*, London: Vintage.

Sabin, Roger (2001), *Comics, Comix and Graphic Novels: A History of Comic Art*, London: Phaidon.

Fifteen Key Works of Contemporary Popular Fiction

1. *The Da Vinci Code* (Dan Brown, 2003)

Dan Brown's conspiracy thriller made him one of the most commercially successful popular fiction writers of the twenty-first century. The novel revolves around dashing Harvard 'Symbologist' Robert Langdon's bid to unravel a murder mystery that involves art history, the Vatican, various cloak-and-dagger organisations and the secret descendants of Jesus Christ. Brown's distinctive (and often parodied) prose style is characterised by short, punchy chapters full of dramatic incident, unlikely plot developments and frequent cliff-hangers. His controversial depiction of the Catholic Church and a high-profile court case during which Brown was accused of breaching copyright by appropriating elements of an earlier work of historical non-fiction only added to the novel's already enormous sales and cultural ubiquity. (Brown won the case.) Brown's most-recent novel, *Inferno*, which, like *Angels and Demons* (2000) and *The Lost Symbol* (2009), again features Robert Langdon, was the best-selling book of 2013.

2. *Let the Right One In / Låt Den Rätte Komma In* (John Ajvide Lindqvist, 2004)

Swedish author Lindqvist's melancholy, resolutely gritty novel – in which a beguiling vampire named Eli who looks 12, but has, she admits, been so, 'for a very long time' moves in next door to a lonely and bullied young boy named Oskar in the run-down suburbs of 1980s Stockholm – is widely considered to be one of the finest horror novels of recent years. In *Let the Right One In*, as in his more recent novels, *Handing the Undead* (2005), *Harbour* (2008) and *Little Star* (2011), Lindqvist reconfigures familiar genre tropes in a manner that acknowledges his obvious debt to authors such as Stephen King, but still has a distinctively Scandinavian sensibility. The novel has already

been filmed twice: first as an internationally acclaimed Swedish version of the same name (2008) and then as an interesting but much less
critically successful American remake (*Let Me In*, 2010).

3. The *Twilight* Saga (Stephenie Meyer, 2005–8)

Meyer's heady tale of the forbidden (and initially chaste) love that
springs up between tormented vampire Edward Cullen (a brooding
perpetual teenager who has been in high school for many decades)
and clumsy, down-to-earth new-girl-in-town Bella Swan, remains one
of the major publishing success stories of the post-2000 era. *Twilight*
and its sequels resonated hugely with both their initial target teen-girl
audience as well as many older female readers, who fiercely identified
with the ups and downs of the lead couple's relationship, and famously
divided themselves into 'Team Edward' and 'Team Jacob'. The success
of the series, as well as its high-profile film adaptations, also lent a
substantial boost to the popularity of the Paranormal Romance sub-
genre, which has been one of the most significant twenty-first century
publishing trends. More recently, Meyer's series inspired E. L. James
to write the fanfiction that evolved into *50 Shades of Grey* (2011).

4. The *Millennium* Trilogy (Stieg Larsson, 2005–7)

In the first volume of Larsson's *Millennium* trilogy, dogged investigative journalist Mikael Blomkvist finds himself opposed to corrupt
and powerful men whose seeming impunity undermines perceptions
that post-war Sweden is an inherently egalitarian social democracy.
Initially published in Swedish as *Män Som Hatar Kvinnor / Men Who
Hate Women* (a title which emphasised Larsson's explicitly feminist
intentions much more than the more obviously 'commercial' English-
language title, *The Girl with the Dragon Tattoo*), the first novel in
the *Millennium* series also introduced readers to the unforgettable
figure of Lisbeth Salander. The bisexual, tattoo-bedecked, troubled
young hacker rapidly became one of the most beloved characters in
contemporary popular fiction. By 2015, the trilogy had sold around
75 million copies. Larsson's series helped kick the so-called 'Nordic
Noir' publishing trend into high gear, and also contributed to the
current crop of pop culture detective figures whose likely placement
somewhere on the autistic/Asperger's spectrum is supposed to contribute to their investigative prowess. A fourth instalment in the series,

published as *The Girl in the Spider's Web* in English, and written by David Lagercrantz, was released in 2015 to generally good reviews and sales of 200,000 in the first week of release alone.

5. *World War Z* (Max Brooks, 2006)

Brooks had previously written the tongue-in-cheek *Zombie Survival Guide* (2003) before turning his hand to this rather more serious take on the walking dead. His stroke of genius in *World War Z* is to use real-life historian Studs Terkel's *'The Good War': An Oral History of World War Two* (1984) as the template for his panoramic account of a devastating 'Zombie War' which almost wipes out humankind. Despite the obviously sensational premise, *World War Z* is a carefully written and thought-provoking exploration of the ways in which sudden catastrophe can violently upend the lives and assumptions of even the most privileged sectors of society. The success of the novel also played a key role in facilitating the recent emergence of 'Zombie Lit' as a distinct publishing category. Largely confined to celluloid before 2000, zombies now populate the pages of countless popular novels, as well as high-profile TV shows, comics and video games.

6. *A Song of Ice and Fire* Series (George R. R. Martin, 1996–)

Martin's series, a gritty secondary-world fantasy about rival factions battling for political and military supremacy in the quasi-medieval setting of the land of Westeros, had already achieved considerable success and secured a significant fan base when the first episode of the TV adaptation, *Game of Thrones*, debuted on HBO in 2011. However, within weeks of the first broadcast, it had become one of the most popular television shows in the world. Martin's series is considered a key work in the 'Grimdark' fantasy movement, a morally complex, mature riposte to what proponents tend to see as the often overly romanticised forms of heroic fantasy inspired by J. R. R. Tolkien. Martin's fiction has changed popular perceptions of heroic fantasy, and significantly widened the themes and subject matters it can encompass, even if some sections of his ardent fan base have of late expressed frustration at the ever-increasing wait between new instalments of the series. Martin is also a respected horror and SF author.

7. The *Harry Potter* Series (J. K. Rowling, 1997–2007)

The huge adult audience that Rowling's tale of a boy wizard with a heroic destiny attracted helped make her seven-volume Harry Potter series one of the most important influences in contemporary publishing. By the time of publication of the final instalment in 2007, it was predicted that teenage and young adult readers would outstrip the number of child readers, in part because those who had started reading the series in 1997 had literally grown up with the series. Rowling's work also helped convince fully grown-up readers that it was perfectly acceptable to read fiction targeted at a YA/children's audience, a trend that has had major implications for the contemporary publishing industry: by 2015, *Publisher's Weekly* was citing the results of a Nielsen survey which showed that 80 per cent of YA titles were being bought by adults. The series may be concluded (for now) in novel form, but at the time of writing, the Potter juggernaut shows no sign of slowing down. In 2016, a film prequel scripted by Rowling, *Fantastic Beasts and Where to Find Them*, was released, and a two-part sequel, a stage play based on a story by Rowling, *Harry Potter and the Cursed Child*, debuted in the West End.

8. The *Hunger Games* Trilogy (Suzanne A. Collins 2008–10)

Collins's gripping and often genuinely grim YA hit took the standard dystopian fiction plot – a heroic individual reluctantly battles against a repressive and seemingly unassailable regime – and reconfigured it for the post 9/11 generation. Youngsters living in Panem, the deeply divided nation built amidst the ruins of what was once the United States, are sacrificed for the entertainment of the masses. Their carefully choreographed suffering is also a means for the tyrannical President Snow to quell discontent amongst the oppressed majority who live in poverty and fear. The series, as Collins has frequently noted, was inspired by a mish-mash of Greek mythology, the Iraq War and reality television. Her notably unsentimental yet uncompromisingly loyal and courageous main character, Katniss Everdeen, soon became a feminist icon, and the book ignited the dystopian YA fiction trend that has only recently peaked. In 2015 it was widely reported upon when economics professor Noreena Hertz dubbed what she called the 'profoundly anxious' cohort of teenage girls born in Britain between 1995 and 2002 'Generation Katniss', because they were apparently shaped by many of the same anxieties regarding technology and existential threat seen in Collins's trilogy.

9. *Pride and Prejudice and Zombies* (Seth Grahame-Smith and Jane Austen, 2009)

Grahame-Smith's inspired fusion of Jane Austen and the living dead (or 'the dreadfuls' as they are called here) constituted one of the most unlikely publishing successes of the early twenty-first century, and helped inspire a rash of other literary 'mash-ups' combining classic nineteenth-century texts with (usually) supernatural horror tropes, as well as a 2016 film adaptation. Though the literary mash-up trend has by and large passed, novels in which Edwardian and Victorian settings and often real-life historical figures encounter fantastical and uncanny threats remain very popular, as evidenced by the current boom in steampunk, and the popularity of TV shows such as *Penny Dreadful* (Showtime, 2014–16).

10. *Ms. Marvel* (G. Willow Wilson and Adrian Alphona)

The superhero known as Ms. Marvel (whose most famous prior incarnation was blonde and blue-eyed air force pilot Carol Danvers) has been part of the Marvel universe since 1977. In 2013, however, Ms. Marvel underwent her most interesting transformation to date when, having acquired superpowers thanks to exposure to mutating 'Terrigen Mists', irrepressible Pakistani-American teenager Kamala Khan adopts the name and becomes the first Muslim character to headline a major comics title. The acclaimed series focuses on Kamala's struggle to juggle family responsibilities, and negotiate clashing cultural expectations. The title also provides a fresh, witty and remarkably fun take on stock superhero tropes. In doing so, the series effectively underlines the positive benefits of increasing gender and racial diversity in popular culture, and demonstrates that consideration of these factors need not render a narrative grimly 'worthy' or reductively tokenistic.

11. *Gone Girl* (Gillian Flynn, 2012)

Flynn's deliciously devious psychological thriller, in which a seemingly perfect marriage is revealed to be anything but, helped establish both the so-called 'Domestic Noir' sub-genre (usually associated with female-written thrillers in which unease and drama comes from intimate relationships) and, more prosaically, the now tiresome trend for novels about grown women with the word 'Girl' featuring prominently in the title. Few of the many authors that have followed in Flynn's wake, however, have her morbid black wit or ability to create uniquely complex – and distinctively unsympathetic – female antagonists. *Gone Girl* protagonist Amy Dunne's acerbic takedown of the so-called 'Cool Girl' character type inspired a thousand think pieces and feminist blog posts, but, characteristically, Amy herself, like Flynn's work more generally, is a lot more nuanced – and much more challenging – than first appearances suggest. Flynn's previous novels – *Sharp Objects* (2006) and *Dark Places* (2009) also feature sardonic female leads for whom intimate relationships (in these instances familial rather than marital) are claustrophobic, intense and potentially deadly.

12. *The Uninvited* (Liz Jensen, 2012)

The emergence of so-called 'Cli-Fi' or 'eco-fiction' represents one of the most interesting developments in popular fiction in recent years. 'Cli-Fi' or 'Climate Change Fiction' has as its most immediately resonant theme the ramifications of global warming, widely considered to be the most serious threat to our long-term survival as a species (the forthcoming zombie apocalypse aside, of course). British author Jensen's novel begins with a series of violent events that initially make it seem a rather standard 'evil child' horror novel, but as the plot progresses it becomes clear that *The Uninvited* is a much more ambitious and, indeed, apocalyptically minded narrative in which the real horror lies in the seemingly inescapable consequences of our own abuse of the natural world. Like Catherine Chanter's *The Well* (2015) and YA titles such as *The Carbon Diaries: 2015* (Saci Lloyd, 2009) and *The Ship* (Antonia Honeywell, 2009), Jensen's novel further illustrates popular fiction's unique ability to dramatise urgent contemporary anxieties in an accessible and effective fashion.

13. *The Southern Reach Trilogy* (Jeff VanderMeer 2014)

The commercial success and critical acclaim afforded VanderMeer's nuanced, disorientating and defiantly original horror/SF/fantasy hybrid – three short and beautifully written novels which chart the progress of bureaucratic and scientific efforts to map an alien landscape that has somehow colonised a coastal region of the US – marks the point at which the emerging fantasy sub-genre known as the 'New Weird' (which is associated with authors such as China Miéville) began to achieve mainstream recognition.

14. *Fifty Shades of Grey* (E. L. James, 2013–15)

James's erotic romance novel began life as *Masters of the Universe*, a work of *Twilight*-inspired fanfiction, before she published it as a serial on her own website. Following e-book publication by a small Australian publishing house under the *Fifty Shades* title, the rights were snapped up by Random House, and by mid-2014 the first novel in the series had already spent a year at the top of the *New York Times* bestseller list. In part thanks to the ability to purchase anonymously offered by e-reading apps, and in part thanks to the word-of-mouth frisson provided by the sadomasochistic practices detailed in the novels (as well as their familiar take on the long-standing romance plots of the 'inexperienced virgin meets charismatic but dangerous older man' sort), *Fifty Shades of Grey* and its sequels became a pop culture sensation, and helped make female-targeted erotic fiction a mainstream publishing phenomenon. The *Fifty Shades* series (which consists of four books at the time of writing) has now sold well over 100 million copies worldwide. The 2015 screen adaptation was critically panned but attracted very large (and again, mainly female) audiences, and the sequel will be released in 2017.

15. *The Martian* (Andy Weir, 2014)

This absorbing (and often very funny) tale of a resourceful astronaut accidentally left stranded on the red planet was initially provided for free download by author Andy Weir on his personal website, before he made it available for sale through Amazon Kindle direct. It was soon one of the site's top science fiction bestsellers, and in 2014 was republished in hard copy by Crown, where it became a major international success. Weir's journey from self-publishing experimentation to mainstream publishing success is one that is becoming increasingly common, as the experiences of writers such as E. L. James, Amanda Hocking, Hugh Howey, Anna Todd and Cassandra Clare attest. Self-publishing provides a means for aspiring authors to build their own audience, and prove the worth of their ideas, without having to approach the traditional publishing gatekeepers first. It is no wonder then that more 'traditional' publishers now keep a close eye on self-published titles that attract a wide audience, with a view to purchasing the rights for themselves. Weir's success, like that of E. L. James, provides further evidence that the future of popular fiction publishing will, ever more frequently, involve making content available over a wide range of digital platforms and formats, as well as in hard copy.

Chronology of Selected Key Dates in Popular Fiction

1764   Publication of *The Castle of Otranto* by Horace Walpole, which provided a blueprint for the classic European gothic novel.

1773   The first collected edition of true crime stories printed under the title *The Newgate Calendar* is published.

1791   Publication of *Charlotte Temple* by Susanna Rowson, one of the first major American bestsellers.

1798   Publication of *Wieland, Or: The Transformation, An American Tale*, by Charles Brockden Brown, the first major American gothic novel.

1813   First publication of *Pride and Prejudice*, by Jane Austen.

1818   Publication of Mary Shelley's *Frankenstein: The Modern Prometheus*, a ground-breaking fusion of gothic and proto-science fiction elements.

1826   Charles Dickens's first novel, *The Pickwick Papers*, is published.

1841   Publication of 'The Murders in the Rue Morgue' by Edgar Allan Poe, which is now recognised as an important precursor to the modern tale of detection.

1846   Publication of first instalment one of the earliest major serialised 'Penny Dreadfuls', *Sweeney Todd*, by James Malcolm Rhymer and Thomas Peckett Prest.

1852   Publication of the anti-slavery novel *Uncle Tom's Cabin* by Harriet Beecher Stowe, the best-selling novel of the nineteenth century.

1860   Establishment in the US of Beadle's Dime Novels – the first wave of cheap, mass-produced paperbacks produced by a so-called 'fiction writing factory'.

1862   Hugely popular 'sensation' novel *Lady Audley's Secret* by Mary Elizabeth Braddon is published.

1868   Publication of *The Moonstone* by Wilkie Collins, which helped establish a prototype for the British detective fiction novel.

1869   Publication of Matthew Arnold's essay collection *Culture and Anarchy*.

1870   The Elementary Education Act provides for the first time for the mass education of working-class children in Britain, and in doing so helps greatly expand the potential reading audience.

1887   First appearance of Sherlock Holmes in Arthur Conan Doyle's *A Study in Scarlet*.

1895   America's first bestseller list appears in the journal *The Bookman*.

1897   Irish author Bram Stoker's *Dracula* is published.

1897   *The War of the Worlds* by H. G. Wells, one of the most influential science fiction stories ever written, appears for the first time in serial form.

1900   The Net Book Agreement, an arrangement between British publishers and booksellers that established fixed pricing for books, and established that they could not be sold to the consumer for less than the officially agreed sum, comes into effect.

1906   The Stratemeyer Syndicate, founded by prolific writer and publisher Edward Stratemeyer, which will dominate children's publishing in the US for decades, is established.

1920   Publication of *The Mysterious Affair at Styles*, the debut novel of future 'Queen of Crime' Agatha Christie.

       First issue of the highly influential pulp magazine *Black Mask* is published.

1923   Establishment of *Weird Tales*, a pulp magazine specialising in tales of fantasy and horror soon associated with authors such as H. P. Lovecraft and Robert E. Howard.

1926   The Book-of-the-Month club is founded in the US.

Publisher and editor Hugo Gernsback establishes the first magazine dedicated to the genre of science fiction, *Amazing Stories*.

1930   Publication of F. R. Leavis's pamphlet 'Mass Civilisation and Minority Culture'.

1931   The *New York Times* bestseller list appears for the first time.

1932   Publication of Q. D. Leavis's *Fiction and the Reading Public*.

1935   The first ever audiobook, a gramophone recording of Agatha Christie's *The Murder of Roger Ackroyd*, is released in the UK.

Penguin Books is founded by publisher Allen Lane.

1937   Superman makes his debut in *Action Comics* first ever issue.

1938   Publication of the best-selling gothic mystery *Rebecca*, by Daphne du Maurier.

1939   Establishment of Pocket Books, which will soon be at the forefront of the mass-market publishing boom in the US.

1944   First publication of *Dialectic of Enlightenment* by Theodor Adorno and Max Horkheimer, in which the term 'culture industry' is coined (it was published in revised form in 1947).

Kathleen Winsor's hugely successful historical romance *Forever Amber* is published.

1949   Harlequin, which will later become the most important publisher of romance fiction in the world, is established in Winnipeg, Canada.

1952   Ian Fleming's *Casino Royale* introduces the world to suave super-spy James Bond.

1954   The first volume of J. R. R. Tolkien's *The Lord of the Rings* epic fantasy trilogy *The Fellowship of the Ring*, is published.

The US Senate subcommittee on juvenile delinquency meets to discuss the allegedly dangerous impact of crime and horror comics titles on their young readers. A self-regulating 'Comics Code' is adopted by the industry.

1956   Debut novelist Grace Metalious's small-town potboiler *Peyton Place* is a publishing sensation.

1964   The term 'graphic novel' is coined by publisher Richard Kyle.

The so-called 'Birmingham School' of Cultural Studies is established in the UK.

1966   The lurid melodrama *Valley of the Dolls*, by Jacqueline Susann, becomes one of the most-talked about 'blockbusters' of all time. Susann becomes the first author to have three books in a row grab the top spot on the *New York Times* bestseller list.

1967   The horror novel *Rosemary's Baby*, by Ira Levin, is published, and helps create the horror-publishing boom of the 1970s and 1980s.

1974   Horror author Stephen King's first published novel, *Carrie*, appears.

The *Sunday Times* bestseller list is established in the UK.

1983   *The Colour of Magic*, British fantasy author Terry Pratchett's first instalment in the long-running *Discworld* series, is published.

1984   Thomas Harris's police procedural/psychological horror novel *Red Dragon* is published, marking the first appearance of the soon-to-be-iconic serial killer Hannibal Lecter.

1986   The first issue of revisionist superhero comic *Watchmen*, written by Alan Moore and drawn by Dave Gibbons, is published by DC comics.

1995   The online book retailing website Amazon.com is launched.

1996   The 'Oprah's Book Club' slot debuts on *The Oprah Winfrey Show*.

UK journalist Helen Fielding's *Bridget Jones's Diary* is published, and helps establish the 'Chick-Lit' sub-genre of romance fiction as a major publishing category.

The first volume of SF/fantasy author George R. R. Martin's epic *A Song of Ice and Fire* series, *A Game of Thrones*, is published.

1997   The Net Book Agreement collapses, ushering in a period of radical restructuring for the publishing industry and for booksellers in the UK, as well as lower prices for consumers.

Harry Potter and the Philosopher's Stone, by J. K. Rowling, is published in the UK. It will be released a year later in the US as *Harry Potter and the Sorcerer's Stone*.

2000   Stephen King's novella *Riding the Bullet* becomes the first mass-market e-book.

2003   Dan Brown's immensely popular conspiracy thriller *The Da Vinci Code* is published.

The first novel designed to be read on a mobile/cell phone is published in Japan.

2005   The first volume in Stephenie Meyer's YA paranormal romance series *Twilight* is published.

The first instalment in Stieg Larsson's *Millennium* trilogy, *Män Som Hatar Kvinnor (Men Who Hate Women)* is posthumously published in his native Sweden.

2006   Self-publishing app Wattpad is launched. As of 2016, it has up to 40 million unique users a month.

2007   The online user-generated book review and recommendation site *Goodreads* is launched.

Amazon's portable e-reading device, the Kindle, goes on sale, enabling users to digitally download books instantly from the company's website. By 2014, Amazon controlled 65 per cent of the e-book market.

Kindle Direct Publishing, which allows authors/publishers to upload their own publications to the Amazon store for purchase on Kindle and Kindle apps, is launched.

2008   Suzanne Collins's *The Hunger Games* helps prompt a boom in dystopian YA fiction.

2009   The satirical 'mash-up' *Pride and Prejudice and Zombies*, by Seth Grahame-Smith and Jane Austen, inspires a multitude of sequels and imitators.

2009   The so-called 'Slender Man' is created by 'Victor Surge' (aka Eric Knudsen) and rapidly becomes a subject of countless 'Creepypasta' stories, photo-shopped images, forum postings and YouTube videos.

US book chain Barnes & Noble launches its 'NOOK' e-reader.

The term 'New Adult Fiction' is coined by St Martin's Press.

2010   Google Books is launched.

2011   US book chain Borders declares bankruptcy.

Erotic romance novel *Fifty Shades of Grey*, by E. L. James, becomes a publishing sensation.

Fantasy/paranormal romance author Amanda Hocking, who had sold one million copies of her self-published fiction (mainly in e-book format) to that date, secures a publishing contract with St Martin's Press.

E-book sales are added to the *New York Times* fiction and non-fiction lists for the first time.

Fortune magazine reports that 20 million e-readers were sold in the US during this year.

According to Forbes, sales of the Kindle reach 13.44 million in 2011. Amazon.com announces that e-book sales have overtaken those of paperbacks for the first time.

2012   Gillian Flynn's psychological thriller *Gone Girl* becomes a major hit on both sides of the Atlantic, and helps establish 'Domestic Noir' as a significant publication category.

The term 'Cli-Fi' ('Climate Change Fiction') enters the mainstream.

2013   The Bowker research group reports that the number of self-published titles has increased five-fold in five years.

2014   The 'We Need Diverse Books' campaign is founded in the US.

2015   Chinese science fiction author Liu Cixin's *The Three-Body Problem* wins the Hugo Award for best novel. The awards are dogged by controversy surrounding supposedly rigged ballots caused by a vocal group of fans and publishers opposed to what they see as the excessive attention paid to issues of race, gender and representation in recent years, the so-called 'Sad Puppies'.

The Association of American Publishers reports a 10 per cent drop in digital sales during 2015, according to *Publisher's Weekly*.

Resurgent UK book chain Waterstones announces that Kindle e-readers will no longer be sold in their stores. It is widely reported that dedicated e-reader sales have dramatically declined in both the UK and the US, in part because of the ubiquity of tablets and smartphones, in addition to higher priced e-books.

Nielsen BookScan reports that e-book sales in the US constitute a 25 per cent market share of total book sales.

Amazon opens its first bricks-and-mortar bookstore in Seattle, amidst media speculation that it will be the first of many.

It is reported that digital audiobooks now represent one of the fastest growing areas of the publishing industry.

2016   Amazon launches the 'Oasis', their smallest and lightest e-reader to date.

Works Cited in A–Z Listing of Key Concepts and Terms

Adorno, Theodor W. (2010), *The Culture Industry: Essays on Mass Culture*, London: Routledge.

Adorno, Theodor W. and Max Horkheimer [1944] (2002), *Dialectic of Enlightenment: Philosophical Fragments*, Stanford: Stanford University Press.

Angenot, Marc (1975), *Le Roman populaire: recherches en paralitterature*, Montreal: Le Presses de l'Universitie du Quebec.

Arnold, Matthew [1869] (2006), *Culture and Anarchy*, Oxford: Oxford University Press.

Ashley, Bob (ed.) (1997), *Reading Popular Narrative: A Source Book*, Leicester: University of Leicester Press.

Beagle, Peter S. (2011), 'Introduction', in Peter S. Beagle and Joe R. Lansdale (eds), *The Urban Fantasy Anthology*, San Francisco: Tachyon Publications, pp. 9–12.

Bloom, Harold (1994), *The Western Canon: The Books and School of the Ages*, New York: Harcourt Brace and Company.

Bloom, Clive (1998), *Cult Fiction: Popular Reading and Pulp Theory*, Basingstoke: Palgrave Macmillan.

Bloom, Clive (2008), *Bestsellers: Popular Fiction since 1990*, Basingstoke: Palgrave Macmillan.

Bolter, Jay David (2001), *Writing Space: Computers, Hypertext, and the Remediation of Print*, Mahwah, NJ: Laurence Erlbaum Associates.

Bourdieu, Pierre (1993), *The Field of Cultural Production: Essays on Art and Literature*, Cambridge: Polity Press.

Bourdieu, Pierre [1979] (1999), *Distinction: A Social Critique of the Judgement of Taste*, London: Routledge.

Brier, Evan (2010), *A Novel Marketplace: Mass Culture, the Book Trade and Postwar American Fiction*, Philadelphia: University of Pennsylvania Press.

Bruhm, Steve (1994), *Gothic Bodies: The Politics of Pain in Romantic Fiction*, Philadelphia: University of Pennsylvania Press.

Busse, Kristina and Karen Hellekson (eds) (2006), *Fan Fiction and Fan Communities in the Age of the Internet*, Trail, NC: McFarland.

Carey, John (2002), *The Intellectuals and the Masses: Pride and Prejudice among the Literary Intelligentsia, 1880–1939*, Chicago: Academy Chicago.

Carroll, Noël (2013), 'The Paradox of Suspense', in P. Vorderer, Hans Jurgen Wuff and Mike Friedrichsen (eds), *Suspense: Conceptualizations, Theoretical Analyses and Empirical Explorations*, London: Routledge, pp. 71–91.

Cawelti, John (1976), *Adventure, Mystery and Romance: Formula Stories as Art and Popular Culture*, Chicago: The University of Chicago Press.

Clute, John and Peter Nicholls (1999), *The Encyclopaedia of Science Fiction*, London: Orbit.

Daly, Nicholas (2000), *Modernism, Romance and the Fin de Siecle: Popular Fiction and British Culture*, Cambridge: Cambridge University Press.

Daly, Nicholas (2012), 'Fiction, Theatre and Early Cinema', in D. Glover and S. McCracken (eds), *The Cambridge Companion to Popular Fiction*, Cambridge: Cambridge University Press, pp. 33–49.

Dalziel, Margaret (1957), *Popular Fiction 100 Years Ago: An Unexplored Tract of Literary History*, London: Cohen and West.

de Certeau, Michel (1984), *The Practice of Everyday Life*, Berkley: University of California Press.

Dorson, Richard M. (1950), 'Folklore and Fakelore', *American Mercury*, vol. 70, pp. 355–443.

Escarpit, Robert (1966), *The Book Revolution*, London: Harrap.

Fiedler, Leslie [1969] (1975), 'Cross the Border – Close the Gap', in *A New Fielder Reader*, New York: Prometheus Books, pp. 270–94.

Fiske, John (1989), *Reading the Popular*, London: Unwin Hyman.

Fiske, John (2010), *Understanding Popular Culture*, London: Routledge.

Gelder, Ken (2010), *Popular Fiction: The Logistics and Practices of a Literary Field*, London: Routledge.

Gilbert, Pamela K. (ed.) (2011), *A Companion to Sensation Fiction*, Oxford: Blackwell.

Hartley, John (2003), *A Short History of Cultural Studies*, London: Sage.

Helgarson, John, Sara Karrholm and Ann Steiner (eds) (2016), *Hype: Bestsellers and Literary Culture*, Lund: Nordic Academic Press.

Hellekson, Karen (ed.) (2001), *The Alternate History: Reconfiguring Time*, Kent, OH: The Kent State University Press.

Hill, Craig (ed.) (2013), 'Introduction: Young Adult Literature and Scholarship Come of Age', in C. Hill (ed.), *The Critical Merits of Young Adult Literature: Coming of Age*, London: Routledge, pp. 1–24.

Hills, Matt (2003), *Fan Cultures*, London: Routledge.

Hoggart, Richard [1957] (2009), *The Uses of Literacy: Aspects of Working Class Life*, London: Penguin Books.

Horowitz, Daniel (2012), *Consuming Pleasures: Intellectuals and Popular Culture in the Postwar World*, Philadelphia: University of Pennsylvania Press.

Horsley, Lee (2010), 'From Sherlock Holmes to the Present', in L. Horsley and C. J. Rzepka (eds), *A Companion to Crime Fiction*, Oxford: Blackwell, pp. 28–42.

Howard, Nicole (2005), *The Book: The Life Story of a Technology*, Westport, CT: Greenwood.

Humble, Nicola (2012), 'The Reader of Popular Fiction', in D. Glover and S. McCracken (eds), *The Cambridge Companion to Popular Fiction*, Cambridge: Cambridge University Press, pp. 86–102.

Hunter, James (1992), *Culture Wars: The Struggle to Control Family, Art, Education, Law and Politics in America*, New York: Basic Books.

Jamison, Anne Elizabeth (2013), *Fic: Why Fan Fiction is Taking Over the World*, Dallas: Smart Pop.

Jenkins, Henry [1993] (2012), *Textual Poachers: Television Fans and Participatory Culture*, New York: Routledge.

Johnson, Deirdre (2011), 'Juvenile Publications', in C. Bold (ed.), *The Oxford History of Popular Print Culture*, Oxford: Oxford University Press, vol. 6, pp. 293–316.

Joshi, S. T. (1990), *The Weird Tale*, Holicong, PA: Wildside Press.

Jumonville, Neil (ed.), *The New York Intellectuals Reader*, New York: Routledge, 2007.

Kolbas, E. Dean (2001), *Critical Theory and the Literary Canon*, Boulder: Westview Press.

Krystal, Arthur (2012), 'Easy Writers: Guilty Pleasures without Guilt', *The New Yorker*, 28 May 2012, online.

le Blanc, Edward T. (2012), 'A Brief History of Dime Novels: Formats and Contents, 1860–1933', in L. C. Sullivan and L. C. Schurman (eds), *Pioneers, Passionate Ladies and Private Eyes: Dime Novels, Series Books and Paperbacks*, London: Routledge, pp. 23–38.

Leavis, F. R. [1930] (2006), 'Mass Civilisation and Minority Culture' in J. Storey, (ed.), *Cultural Theory and Popular Culture: A Reader*, Harlow: Pearson, pp. 12–21.

Leavis, Q. D. [1932] (1979), *Fiction and the Reading Public*, Harmondsworth: Penguin.

Lindner, Christopher (2014), 'Foreword', in R. Allen and T. van den Berg (eds), *Serialisation in Popular Culture*, London: Routledge, pp. ix–xi.

McCloud, Scott (1994), *Understanding Comics: The Invisible Art*, New York: HarperCollins.

McCracken, Scott (1998), *Pulp: Reading Popular Fiction*, Manchester: Manchester University Press.

McCracken, Scott (2004), 'The Half-Lives of Literary Fictions: Genre Fictions in the Late-Twentieth Century', in L. Marcus and P. Nicholls (eds), *The Cambridge History of Twentieth-Century English Literature*, Cambridge: Cambridge University Press, pp. 618–34.

Macdonald, Dwight [1960] (2011), *Masscult and Midcult: Essays against the American Grain*, New York: New York Review of Books.

Matterson, Stephen (2003), *American Literature: The Essential Glossary*, London: Arnold.

Meyhoff, Karsten Wind (2012), 'Freak Ecology: An Introduction to the

Fictional History of Natural Disaster', in C. Meiner and K. Veel (eds), *The Cultural Life of Catastrophes and Crises*, Berlin: Walter de Gruyter, pp. 295–308.

Mort, John (2002), *Christian Fiction: A Guide to the Genre*, Santa Barbara: Libraries Unlimited.

Nash, Walter (1990), *Language in Popular Fiction*, London: Routledge.

Neuburg, Victor E. (1977), *Popular Literature: A History and Guide*, London: Penguin.

Newman, Kim (1999), *Millennium Movies: End of the World Cinema*, London: Titan.

Pawling, Christopher (ed.) (1984), *Popular Fiction and Social Change*, London: Macmillan Press.

Philips, Deborah (2006), *Women's Fiction 1945–2005: Writing Romance*, London: Routledge.

Ramsey, Colin T. and Kathryn Zabelle Derounian-Stodola (2004), 'Dime Novels', in S. Samuels (ed.), *A Companion to American Fiction 1780–1865*, Oxford: Blackwell, pp. 262–73.

Ross, Trevor (1998), *The Making of the English Literary Canon: From the Middle Ages to the Late Eighteenth Century*, Montreal: McGill-Queen's University Press.

Rothman, Joshua (2014), 'A Better Way to Think about the Genre Debate', *The New Yorker*, 6 November, online.

Russ, Joanna (1995), 'Somebody's Trying to Kill Me and I Think It's My Husband: The Modern Gothic', in J. Russ, *To Write Like a Woman: Essays on Feminism and Science Fiction*, Bloomington: Indiana University Press, pp. 94–119.

Seltzer, Mark (1998), *Serial Killers: Life and Death in America's Wound Culture*, New York: Routledge.

Server, Lee (2009), *Encyclopaedia of Pulp Fiction Writers*, New York: Infobase Publishing.

Sobral, Ana (2012), *Opting Out: Deviance and Generational Difficulties in American Post-War Cult Fiction*, Amsterdam: Rodopi.

Stableford, Brian (2006), *Science Fact and Science Fiction: An Encyclopaedia*, London: Routledge.

Storey, John (2009), *Cultural Theory and Popular Culture: An Introduction*, London: Pearson and Longman.

Storey, John (2010), *Cultural Studies and the Study of Popular Culture*, Edinburgh: Edinburgh University Press.

Sutherland, John (2007), *Bestsellers: A Very Short Introduction*, Oxford: Oxford University Press.

Swann, Steven Jones (2013), *The Fairy Tale*, London: Routledge.

Thompson, John B. (2010), *Merchants of Culture: The Publishing Business in the Twenty-First Century*, Cambridge: Polity.

Todorov, Tzvetan (1975), *The Fantastic: A Structural Approach to a Literary Genre*, Ithaca, NY: Cornell University Press.

Todorov, Tzvetan (1977), 'The Typology of Detective Fiction', in *The Poetics of Prose*, New York: Cornell University Press, pp. 49–52.

VanderMeer, Ann and Jeff VanderMeer (eds) (2008), *The New Weird*, San Francisco: Tachyon Publications.

VanderMeer, Ann and Jeff VanderMeer (eds) (2011), *The Weird: A Compendium of Strange and Dark Stories*, London: Atlantic Books.

Weaver-Zercher, Valerie (2013), *Thrill of the Chaste: The Allure of Amish Romance Novels*, Baltimore: The Johns Hopkins University Press.

Whissen, Thomas R. (1992), *Classic Cult Fiction: A Companion to Popular Cult Literature*, Westport, CT: Greenwood Press.

White, Curtis (2004), *The Middle Mind: Why Americans Don't Think For Themselves*, London: Penguin.

Whiteside, Thomas (1981), *The Blockbuster Complex: Conglomerates, Showbusiness, and Book Publishing*, Middletown, CT: Wesleyan University Press.

Williams, Raymond (1975), 'Introduction', in *Marxism and Literature*, Oxford: Oxford University Press, pp. 1–10.

Williams, Raymond (1977), *Marxism and Literature*, Oxford: Oxford University Press.

Zidle, Abby (1999), 'From Bodice-Ripper to Babysitter: The New Hero in Mass-Market Romance', in A. K. Kaler and Rosemary E. Johnson Kurek (eds), *Romantic Conventions*, Bowling Green, OH: Popular Press, pp. 23–34.